MONEY
TO
START A
BUSINESS

How To Raise All The Money You'll Ever Need To Start Your Own Business

by Perry Belcher

Library of Congress Catalog –PENDING

Belcher, Perry.

Money to Start a Business: How To Raise all the

Money You'll Ever Need to Start Your Own

Business / by Perry Belcher

p. cm.

Includes bibliographical references and index.

ISBN 978-1-937126-99-5

    1. Business

Title.

PN151.B4556 2011

808'.02023—dc22

About The Author

Perry Belcher is a serial entrepreneur, author, publisher, copywriter, marketer, SEO expert, importer and business coach from Austin, Texas.

Perry has imported, manufactured, created and sold more than $100,000,000 in merchandise, information and services over his career.

Perry is an author of 11 books and courses on business in just the past few years.

He is also a devoted husband and father to two daughters and two sons, and the worst guitar player in all of Texas.

Today, Perry is semi-retired and spends most of his time these days consulting with and investing in mid-sized businesses where he can add the greatest value.

In addition, Perry has been a keynote speaker at many business and marketing functions.

To hire Perry, please contact Sandy Bradshaw at 512-555-1212

Contact Perry through social media

twitter.com/perrybelcher
perrybelcher.com/facebook
youtube.com/perrybelcher

or read Perry's blog at perrybelcher.com

Contents

This guide is going to explain how to raise money for your new business. It's is an exciting time for you as a brand-new business owner, getting started and raising the cash that you need to expand your business, grow your business, take it to a local level or national stage.

Whatever you're trying to do, I'm going to try to help you raise money for your business through multiple sources: everything from private equity; friends and family; angel investors all the way up to venture capitalist SBA loans; and everything else.

Disclaimer

Before we get started, I have to clarify a couple of things. Number one, income claims: if at any time you think that I'm implying that if you do a certain thing you're guaranteed to get funding or you're guaranteed to make a certain amount of money, that's just not true. I don't make any income claims, I don't make any guarantees that you're going to get a loan or you're going to get funded for your business. That would be impossible to say based on the fact I don't have any idea what you're doing or the amount of effort you want to put in.

Number two: I'm going to describe certain legal issues, corporation formations, things like that. You definitely need to consult with your local attorney before doing any of these things. I'm not giving you any legal advice; I am not a licensed professional in any field, especially not law or accounting. You'll definitely want to seek out professionals in your own local market to help you with those particular needs. Everyone's legal needs are different and I couldn't possibly know your situation. What I tell you here is broad-based knowledge, meant for information purposes only.

Getting Money 1

I've bootstrapped a lot of businesses in the past.
I've had the privilege of going through the SBA
lending process through a partner. I've dealt with
venture capital firms; I've dealt with angel
investors, private offerings. I even got very near to
taking a company public, so I've dealt with pretty
much all the stages of financing that you can go
through. I've been involved in about thirteen start-
up companies over the past years. I hate to say
how old I am now. My start-up days are starting to
wind up. I'm going to hopefully be on the investor
side of the table pretty soon. That's basically what
happens to us old guys.

I've dealt with a lot of these. I know a lot of VC
people. I know a lot of people that are investors in
businesses, angel investors, small investors in

businesses, people who have dealt with a loan process over time, and I know a lot about what they're looking for.

More importantly, though, I know what they're not looking for: the reasons people won't loan you money, won't fund your project, or won't invest. Most of the time, this is more important than why they will. If you know their red flags, you have a big advantage.

Why To Raise Money

There are a lot of reasons you need to raise money, but the biggest reason is the single largest reason businesses fail: under-capitalization. Most people who start a business don't have the proper amount of funds to get through the learning curve of the business. Especially if people haven't run a business before; if you're brand-new to something, you're definitely going to have a learning curve. It takes a period of time, typically, to acquire customers, establish vendor relationships, things like that. You're sort of raising money to buy time. A lot of the time you need assets, you need equipment, you need particular things that require tools for your business that you're going to have to raise money for depending on what you're doing. The reason to raise money is to pay for those things if you don't have the money to do it yourself.

Why Not To Raise Money

The reasons why not are twentyfold. There are a ton of them. When you borrow money from somebody, whether in a loan or a company, by taking in an investor, even if you just borrow money from rich Aunt Marge: this money comes with strings and sometimes Aunt Marge can be harder to deal with than the venture capital companies.

Running a business is hard. Starting a business is harder. When you're starting a business, having to deal with it, you have a whole other element to deal with in an investor or a funding partner. They're going to be something that takes part of your time. They're actually partners with you now. Once they're investing in your business, they basically become your partner.

You're going to have to answer to performance milestones if you're dealing with angel investors or venture capital companies, and even a lot of loans. Along your financing path, they're going to want to know how things are going, what's going on. There is going to be a lot of reporting. The more transparent you are with them, the better they're going to feel about you. "Hey, I'm just too busy," isn't going to work. If a guy or lady's got their hard-earned money on the line with you, when they want to talk to you and find out how things are going, they expect you to stop and tell them.

Working With Your Investors

You always want to be honest with whoever you're working with. I think the biggest problem that I see when most people have conflicts with their lenders or their investors is a lack of transparency, not letting people know what's going on. It's a lack of communication. Angel investors and venture capital investors are what I call 'smart money investors'. A lot of the time what you get from them in money is the smallest part of the deal. They become your partners. All of a sudden you're a partner with somebody who is experienced, who has connections, who knows talented people, who has, in most cases, been there and done that. Most of these people that are working in venture capital funds, especially angel investors (less so venture capital funds, although they all have an element of it), are entrepreneurial. They're usually former entrepreneurs or former business owners, so they were where you are. They understand, so talk to them. Not only will you gain their trust by being transparent and honest with them, you'll probably get the answers to a lot of problems that are just perplexing you.

When To Ask For Funding

Picking the right time to ask for funding is probably the biggest mistake that people who raise money make. Believe it or not, there aren't as many entrepreneurs out there as there are investors. That sounds hard to imagine. Being an entrepreneur is not just a skill: you bring energy to people who are out of energy, out of ideas, but have capital to invest and want to make it earn. They're pretty shrewd.

It's all based on what your company is worth. If your company is an idea on the back of a napkin, it's not worth much, so they don't expect to give you much money. The further along you've gone in the process, especially testing your model and proving your theories, the more money you're going to be able to raise and the less equity you're going to need to give up.

Ways To Raise Capital   2

In most traditional businesses, there are five ways
to raise money. I'll describe these briefly and then
we'll go on to cover each of them in extreme
detail.

Robbing Your Piggy Bank

Number one is 'robbing your piggy bank'.
Basically your own money and instruments that
you own that convert to money. Cash savings, your
house, taking a second mortgage on your home,
credit cards, take money out of your 401k,
borrowing against your 401k at work, whatever.
It's putting your own money at risk, taking money
out of your own pocket and putting it at risk.

I'll take this point right now and say if you're not
willing to do that at a pretty substantial level, if

you're not willing to risk financially to move towards your venture, you're really not at a point right now that you should ask other people to do that. If you don't believe in what you're doing enough to risk your own capital, it's unlikely anybody else is going to be willing to risk capital for you, especially if you're going to angel investors and venture capital companies. If you don't have some skin in the game, they're not going to be very interested in what you have to show them. If you don't believe in it enough to have your own money invested in it, they certainly are not going to jump into the wagon to get on there with you. Make sure that you've made up your mind, that you believe in what you're doing enough that you're willing to risk some of your own money to put money in the game.

Friendly Investors

The second step is friends and family. Aren't you excited about going to see your dad to tell him: "Dad, I have this great business idea and I just need $10,000"? Or your mom or your rich Aunt Marge or whoever. Now you have a new partner that knows you better than just about anybody does! I'd almost rather have a venture capital partner than have my rich aunt funding a business deal for me. That's just a matter of preference.

I call them 'friendly investors'. This is different from angel investors; a lot of people get those terms confused and think that an 'angel investor' is a rich relative that loans them money to start a business. That's not really true.

Most friends and family are going to loan you money. There are fun ways to do this. You can have big parties, fund-raising parties. I've seen guys do really well with that. Your friends and family are typically going to loan you money for your business because they like you, because they know you, because they want to help you and see you succeed. Their biggest objective is probably getting their principle loan back. If Aunt Marge loans you $10,000 and she gets her $10,000 back sometime in the near future, she's probably going to be thrilled, tickled pink. She's not necessarily going to look for a $30,000 or $40,000 return on her $10,000 investment.

Traditional Loans

Third is traditional loans. People-loaned money, believe it or not, is usually much, much less expensive than equity money is. To take out a loan to start your business is usually considerably less expensive than going to angel investors or venture capital companies.

The problem is, most local banks don't really make business loans anymore, other than those that are guaranteed by the Small Business Administration, the SBA. Most business people have heard about SBA loans before and don't know a lot about them. What you hear from most people when you ask about an SBA loan, is:

> "Oh yeah, you get an SBA loan, but you're going to have to fill out all the paperwork in the world. You're going to have to have tons of collateral, you're going to have to wait forever."

They're right on the first, second, and third points. All three of those are true, except in just the last couple of years, the SBA has put in a new program called SBA Express. It's really exciting. They give you a loan decision within 36 hours.

SBA, by the way, doesn't make loans. They're just a guarantee agency, but they work with local banks. They'll make you a loan decision within 36 hours, and you can be funded within a week. With certain programs they have, you can go up to $500,000 without having to have a whole lot of collateral to back it up if you have decent credit. Your credit doesn't have to be sterling. It just has to be pretty good.

Traditional loans are definitely a route that I think a lot of entrepreneurs are going back to and taking a hard look at again. Loans are really good for stable industries. If you want to start a produce stand and you know that you can make money with produce stands, maybe you're going to have three or four produce stands, a loan is a really much better way to go.

You're going to have a hard time getting angel investors or venture capital companies excited about your produce stand, unless you've totally invented a new way to sell produce. For the most part, those are slow-growth, stable industries. What angel investors and venture capital companies like are fast-growth industries, things that are really fast-paced. You hear so much about technology deals and Silicon Valley and bio deals and energy deals and things like that. Markets that move very quickly are what the angel investors really like.

Back to SBA again. Don't expect to go down to your local banker and say, "Hey, I want to start up a business, why don't you give me $100,000?" They're just going to ask you, "What are you going to put up that's worth $150,000?" in case you don't make the loan. SBA helps you with that.

Angel Investors

Fourth is my favorite way of funding businesses: angel investors. Angel investors are basically like your rich Aunt Marge, but they want a considerable return on their investment, anywhere from three to ten times what they invested in your company. It sounds pretty expensive, and it is. It's a lot more expensive than loan money, but they bring a lot to the table and you'll understand why in a few minutes when we get down to that section.

Angel investors and venture capital investors get mixed up a lot. There's a great distinction between a venture capital company and an angel investor, and that is the angel investor is investing their own money. They had to earn it, inherit it, whatever they did. Most of the time, angel investors are taking a small percentage of what they have in net worth and they're investing it in small companies.

We'll talk about why they do it in a minute, but the main reason they do it is because it's fun. They like being in the entrepreneurial circle, especially older investors that have been out of business for a while. They have a lot of money, and they want the excitement and the fun of a start-up, but they don't want to actually have to do the start-up work. Angel investors are a great source of funding.

Angel investors have groups, too. Sometimes you'll be dealing with an angel investor group where ten or twelve angel investors get together and they form a firm together. They either invest their money collectively or individually, or they bring you in, you do a pitch, tell them what you want to do. The firm makes a decision as a group whether or not they're going to fund you, and then they take group funds and fund you, or three of the angel investors out of ten may say, "We'll take this deal," and the other seven will pass. It's very common in the angel investor world for that to happen. One of the good things is if you get to the point where you're pitching in front of ten, 12 people, your odds of striking a chord with one of them are pretty good. If you have chinks in your armor or flaws in your business plan, these guys are experienced and they're going to find it.

Venture Capitalists

Venture capital companies are the last thing on my list, and actually the last place I'd go when seeking funding unless you know you have a project that's going to take multiple millions of dollars, and you have something that's very, very revolutionary, I would wait a little while before I go to a venture capital company.

Venture capital companies are like angel investors, but instead of investing their own money, they are investing other people's money, so they can't take quite the same risks. A venture capitalist manages money for people who are willing to make high-risk investments for high return. Typically, they're managing money for pension funds, corporations, individuals that say:

> "Okay, I'll give you 1% or 2% of my total portfolio to manage in your venture capital fund, but I'm going to expect this ridiculous return back from it."

These venture capital companies don't loan money, they actually buy equity. They have to put money in play. If they don't put money in play, they're typically not going to earn the returns that their fund contributors expect. Nobody ever believes me when I tell them this, but there is far, far more capital out there in the world right now that's looking for a home than there are viable deals. There aren't as many viable deals as there is capital by probably a 20:1 ratio. There's probably twenty times more money out there that wants to invest in you but can't do it unless you have all your ducks in a row, because the guys that run those funds make a lot of money, they have nice, big, fat, cushy jobs, and they don't want to lose them. If they lose money for their investors, they lose reputation, they lose contributors, and pretty soon that fund's gone, and they lose their fat-cat jobs.

That's basically the five sources that I've seen used and have used myself personally in the past to raise capital for my company.

A Good Idea? 3

How do you know if you have a worthwhile idea?
A while back I was watching TV, and that
American Inventor TV show was on. Of course,
everybody on there thinks they have the best idea,
but there was one guy that had dropped about
$100,000 of his own personal money. He was
sleeping in the back of his car, he had lost his wife,
and when he got in front of the judges they told
him his idea wasn't worth squat. How does you
make sure that doesn't happen to you?

Why Go Into Business?

Most people decide they're going to go into a
business for a couple reasons. They either come up
with a killer idea (or what they *believe* is a killer
idea) or their friends or family tell them that
something they're doing is a really great idea.

I have a friend that makes these Cajun hams that are just amazing. I've been trying to talk him into going into business forever because he makes these delicious hams in the holidays for all his friends and family.

A lot of the time your friends or family will say "Man, you're really good at this," or "This widget you came up with to hold leaves when you're raking them in the yard is just incredible, you should sell that." Most of the time people get the slightest little bit of encouragement, and they have their idea and they're off and running. Some people are just inventive. It's just the way that some are built.

Test Your Friends

I have a couple of tests that I like to give. Everybody always asks their friends' opinions, especially if they're in a specialty industry, "What do you think of this?" Ninety-nine times out of a hundred, the person's going to say, "Oh, man, that's a great idea. That's a really great idea. I like that."

Next ask them, "Well, what do you think a service or product like that would be worth?" If they say, "I think that'd be worth $100," you say, "Okay, cool! I'll make you the first prototype for $50. Would you like me to make one for you?"

If they say, "Absolutely, man! Do it, right now! I'll take it." Then you probably have a reasonable idea. If they hem and haw at that point after they've told you how great your thing is, they're the best customer you're probably ever going to have. They're your friend, they've already talked good things about you, and if they hem and haw and aren't willing to reach in their back pocket at that point, you probably have a problem.

You should then tell them, "You know, I was doing that kind of as a test, and my idea failed the test. You didn't fail the test. Why didn't you like it?" They're probably a little more frank with you then.

Do Your Homework

Try that with more people. Give your product away. If it's a physical product you're making, make some of them and give them away to people. See if they use them. See if they like them. See what your feedback is. Most people just don't do that. We kid about it around here, the *if-we-build-it-they-will-come* mentality.

Web businesses are horrible for it. You know, "We're going to build this amazingly killer website." I have a neighbor right now who's a very smart guy, was a high-paid executive at WorldCom, and he's built this amazing website. It does a lot of neat stuff, but he has no plan for how he's going to get visitors to it. He has no idea how he's going to gain a single first visitor to come to the website.

A lot of people will decide they're going to open a restaurant. Let's say they're going to open a restaurant and they're going to go place it on a certain street, and they'll just arbitrarily pick a space by what's available. It's not by the demographic value, the real estate, how many cars drive by a day, how many of the people are Italian-American and if they're selling Italian food, how many people are within the prime age to dine out. They don't do all the demographic homework.

That's the reason you're seeing Mom and Pop retailers evaporate. They don't exist anymore because these major corporations spend a lot of time in demographics. Find out if they'd buy it first.

If you're selling a food item, take it out and let people taste it. If you have a new website that you're going to charge $1,000 a month for, find ten influential people in your industry and let them have access to it for free. Just beg them to use it. Don't try to sell it to them or anything. Just say, "I'm begging you to use this thing, see what you think of it, tell me how it sucks. I don't want to hear how great it is. I want to hear what's wrong with it, try to make it better."

Red Flags

That being said, there are a couple things that are flags for me and are flags for investors. People come up to you and say, "Oh man, I have something that everybody needs!" Most investors are going to take a walk from that, because there aren't that many things that we need in life. If you think about it, the basics of life are food, shelter, transportation, are all reasonably inexpensive, and they're all very competitive. You look at ten houses on a street and most of them are within $10,000 of one another. There's nothing that makes them stand out.

People spend a lot more money on what they *want*. People will spend insane money on what they want. They don't rationalize shop or justify their purchases much for something that they want versus something that they need. I have on a Rolex watch right now. Would a $20 watch tell time? Would it function the same way? Yes, it would, but I like this watch. I wanted this watch. I certainly didn't need it. So who is more profitable, Rolex or Timex? I would guess that Rolex is a more profitable corporation for sure. People spend a lot more money on what they want. When you're talking to your potential investors, be sure to focus on what people want.

Another big red flag that goes off in my head is, "Oh man, I have this thing and everybody wants it, and there's no competition!" That typically just shows your ignorance. There's almost always competition in any market. When you say that to an investor, they're going to look at you like you're from Mars and try to get away from you just as quickly as they possibly can.

If there aren't any competitors, it's going to scare them even more. If you're really telling the truth and there really aren't any competitors, that's probably because people have tried and failed miserably. We live in a nation of millions of entrepreneurs who fill every possible crevice of the economic landscape. When there's an opportunity, there's almost always somebody that's found an angle at that opportunity.

Revolutionary Or Incremental?

You have to determine if your business is going to be revolutionary or incremental; if your development is a revolutionary product, or an incremental improvement on a currently existing product. Most people believe whatever they're selling is revolutionary. The guy on American Inventor probably thought his thing was absolutely revolutionary.

If anything, revolutionary ideas are like home run hitters in baseball. You swing a lot, you get out a lot, but occasionally you hit a home run. That's not, for the most part, what angel investors or venture capital companies are looking for because the risk associated to the ones that miss, the strike-outs, typically bomb miserably. They just absolutely tank.

Occasionally, somebody hits it out of the ballpark. There are companies out there, like Sequoia Capital and other massive venture capital firms, that have a lot of money to take smart risks, and who know what revolutionary developments are. What is really neat is what could happen if you hit one that will take risks. If you have something revolutionary, by all means, I encourage you.

Know this: if you have something truly revolutionary that could change people's lives for the better, then you have something of immense value. Don't let that be discounted or give away a big portion of it. The companies that you need, if you find the right ones, will be willing to pay you infinite amounts of money to help you develop your idea.

But also know this: most of the time, ideas are not revolutionary. Most of the time they're incremental, and that's okay. The Dyson vacuum cleaner is an incremental improvement on the Hoover vacuum cleaner. It has a different mechanism; it does the same thing. The vacuum cleaner is not particularly revolutionary. It sucks up stuff out of the carpet. It's the way that it does it and the fact that it doesn't clog up and the fact that it pivots around corners and all those things that weren't in a vacuum cleaner before make that particular vacuum cleaner an incremental improvement, and leads the pack of quality in the vacuum cleaner world.

Maybe you've seen the commercials for the Will It Blend Blender. It has a three-horsepower motor and it'll blend up an oil can, or whatever. Like you'd need to blend up an oil can. But the point that it's better than the other blenders is really cool. I want you to think about this.

Markets With Flawed Competition

The very best place for angel investors, venture capitalists and investors looking for ROI is if you can show that you're going into a market where the competition just sucks. They're doing a lousy job, and your solution is way, way better. It's cheaper, it's easier to deliver, and the people who are in the business right now, they have all these flaws and all these things screwed up with their business. If they're still making money and quite a lot of money, that's where you're going to get an investor really turned on.

There's a lot of stuff like that out there. They've proven the model already. If you look at all the search engines that came along before Google, I'm sure that Google took into account everything that was wrong with every other search engine, all the hiccups. The thing was, back in the day, almost all

46

those search engines were making money. They were making bucks. Google had an easy sales pitch. They went in and said, "Look, we have the perfect search engine. It doesn't have any of these things wrong with it. This is our vision, this is what we're going to do." They had a grandiose scale on what they wanted to do. Even though Google is a revolutionary company with some of the things they've done now, their initial business model was not at all revolutionary. It was incremental.

It's a good idea to find a market where the initial trail has been blazed but it hasn't been totally cleared yet. If you can find a growth industry, somewhere that you can go, something that's just a hot industry right now that's moving quickly, and you go "Man, that's really great, but it needs this thing."

Not to get too far into the tech sector, but I do a lot of PowerPoint presentations, and there was a company called Omnisio. They had a video on the right and your PowerPoint presentation ran in sync on the left while you were talking. It was a big, widescreen video that played on computers. We found that so cool because we wanted to do presentations with video. They put out their service as a free service. The company was only in business for four months and they were acquired just the end of last month by Google for a reported $15 to $20 million, cash. The owners of the company are now on the Google team. All they did was add PowerPoint slides to YouTube, fundamentally. They added a feature that made online video better. That was a really sexy incremental change.

The bigger the step, the more money you get. The wheel was around for a long time and somebody put a tire on it. That was a pretty big incremental step. It didn't mean that it wasn't still just a wheel. It was just a wheel with rubber on it. But that incremental step made a big difference in people's comfort and durability and safety and everything else.

A lot of people will change the packaging on a product and say "Oh, look, it's revolutionary!" That's marketing. That's rinse and repeat. That's not really an incremental change. Most VC firms or venture capital firms and angel investors are going to see that as marketing.

Now, where is that important? If you have an industry that's making a product, let's say, and everybody in the industry has lousy packaging, and everybody in the industry ships late, and everybody in the industry does whatever, there can be an incremental product made in the model itself. Dominoes pizza didn't invent pizza. They invented "Pizza in 30 minutes or less or it's free."

They had a killer message. They had a model: "We deliver super-fast but if the customers don't get it in time, we give their money back." They didn't even claim the pizza was good. Their message just said, "Hot pizza delivered in 30 minutes or less or it's free."

Papa John's was the one that came in and said "Better ingredients." It's a pretty weak claim, actually, to build that company as well as its built. But they have pretty good pizza. I hope you understand the difference between revolutionary and incremental. Somebody's building an electric car. That's still really just an incremental change. It's not revolutionary. If you've come up with a vehicle that floats on air, now that's a revolutionary change. The fact that the motor's different in the car does not make the car different. It's still a car. See what I mean? That would be a major incremental change. Just know that most things you're going to come up with are going to be incremental and not revolutionary, and that's okay.

Robbing Your Piggy Bank 4

Most businesses I've started have been bootstrap businesses. With the exception of the super-smart, gifted programmer that writes the killer app or the weird scientist that discovers the cure for some disease or something like that, most people start off their businesses in a bootstrap stage.

That means that basically, you're going to come up with the money to create your business plan and to do all your market research, to get everything ready for your business to get started. You're probably going to come up with it out of your own pocket. Almost nobody's going to fund you or give you the money to research or to develop a plan.

It's something that really doesn't take a lot of cash. It takes a lot of learning and time. It may take some cash to do some prototyping and things like that and to get the information that you need.

I'm going to give you some sources of bootstrap money you might not have thought of. You can bootstrap your entire process, and this is a big revelation to a lot of people, if you plan on owning this business for decades or years and you've said, "This is what I want to do with my life, and for the next 20 years I want to open this store and I want to retire in it."

Your venture capital partners or angel investor partners are not going to feel that way. Most angel investors and venture capital companies invest money with an end in mind. They're looking for a liquidity event, they call it, where somewhere along the way they either get bought out, you go public, or you sell, you get acquired. If you're going down the route of start-up and you want to raise money for business and you don't really want to be out of that business, or you don't want to sell it in a year or two, then the bootstrapping is probably going to be your best way to go.

Bootstrapping

Bootstrapping basically means taking the money that you have: the cash you have stuffed under the mattress; of course, savings accounts are one of the first places we go; taking a second mortgage on your home is very common, or a first mortgage if you don't have a mortgage. Also, you can refinance your automobile, if it's close to being paid off, to get some cash to work with.

People cringe when I say this, but more businesses start on credit cards than anything else. I have a friend of mine now that has cash flowing in business: $150,000 on credit cards right now. Is that a risky thing to do? Of course it is. It's certainly a risky thing to do. American Express cards are pretty awesome for working with business owners and entrepreneurs. They understand what the entrepreneur needs. There are other credit cards that, if you have good credit and can build a good credit rating, want to give you all the credit they can. It's hard to get a $100,000 credit card. It's not hard to get ten $10,000 credit cards, oddly enough.

Robert Townsend made his first movie as a director and producer and he did it all on credit cards. He spent about $100,000 to make his first movie, and now he's a very famous director. That story of the credit cards was a big story.

Tax refunds: people don't think about that. A lot of people have tax refunds. You can take a tax refund loan. If you know you're going to have a tax refund at the end of the year, there are some places now that will give you a tax refund loan earlier in the year rather than at the end of the year so that you can get your hands on some of that cash now.

If you're working where you have a 401k plan, you can typically borrow against that 401k plan or liquidate that 401k plan. There's usually a penalty if you liquidate it. There's not usually a penalty if you borrow against it. If you have a life insurance policy that you've had for a long time, they may have cash value and you may be able to cash those in or take loans against your life insurance policies. If you have stock accounts or any kind of trading accounts, you can typically borrow against those accounts, low-interest.

I've seen students take excess of what they have left over from student loans and start businesses. That happens all the time. I can't legally give you the advice to do that, because I don't know that it's legal. I don't know that it's not legal, I don't know. But a lot of people do that. If you excess your tuition and things like that, I would assume you can do anything you want to do with that money, but I'm not sure. Better check on that. But student loan money is common.

Things that people don't think about: life insurance is one, there's stuff like refinancing your cars, selling boats, selling motorcycles, selling four-wheelers, selling jet-skis. Have a cash-raising eBay sale, or a cash-raising yard or garage sale where you just take everything that you don't really need in life and sell it.

Have Skin In The Game

This sounds like I'm telling you to be a fanatic, but if you're going to plan to succeed in business right now, you'd better get fanatic. This is a competitive landscape no matter what you're doing anymore. Businesses are getting more competitive. You have to be ready to buckle down. If you cut that net out from under you, you make it painful to retreat. Make it painful to fail. If it becomes too easy to fail, you're more likely to fail.

Imagine if you go to your family and your friends (which is the next step we're going to get to) and ask to raise funds from them. If they know that you've second-mortgaged your house, you've maxed out your credit cards, you've cashed in your life insurance, you've sold your boat, your car, your motorcycle, everything, they know that you believe. They're going to catch onto your believing. If they know that you're absolutely that committed, the chances of them wanting to help you and participate are much, much higher. Having skin in the game gets you a lot of points.

Keep Records

One little thing that I'll throw in here real quick is to document everything that you spend on the business. If you cash in a life insurance policy and put it in a business account, document it. You're going to want to go in someday to a venture capital company or to an angel investor or someone else and say:

> "Hey, look. Here's my list. I have $75,425.15 invested of my own money. Here's the documentation proving it. Here's where I put it in. This is what I've taken out."

Most people don't think about documenting all of that stuff as they're putting it in. Always, another little tip for keeping books and records: start keeping really clear easy books right away. I don't care if you keep them on a ledger pad; you want to document everything that comes in and everything that goes out and classify it. The single biggest reason that you won't get the maximum amount of money when you go to get funded is because you have poor books and records. That is usually the number one reason.

Show Your Commitment

Most people don't go to angel investors or venture capitalists with the right kind of data. Especially if they're not familiar with how the game is played. If you follow the instructions in this guide, it's going to put you above 90-95% of the pack. Most people who go to venture capital firms to pitch are totally unprepared. They think, "I have a good idea and these people have money, combine the two and we're going to go set the world on fire and get rich!"

That ain't the way the game's played. They have rules. You're walking in a room to meet these people, a bunch of strangers, saying: "Hi, my name is Perry. Get out your checkbook and give me a couple hundred thousand dollars, or a couple million dollars." That's a pretty doggone ballsy assumption, you know? You need to start establishing trust from that very first moment:

> "Hi. Each of you has a folder in front of you. This is proof of what I have invested in the business so far. I just want to show you that is everything I have pretty much is in that folder in front of you right now. I have everything to lose."

That really goes a long way. Think about that versus the guy that doesn't do that. The contrast is dramatic. They know you're committed. If you spewed out an idea that is commercially not viable, that's not going to help you. It doesn't matter. But if your idea is commercially viable and the next guy comes in and his idea is commercially viable, you're definitely going to have an advantage.

It seems that a lot of people have a good idea but haven't put in the skin and they want somebody else to do the work for them. In this kind of situation where you go in front of venture capitalists or angel investors, it would really do you well to think in terms of what they want more than what you want.

Here is the big picture, basically. The best situation you can be in when standing in front of an investor is to say:

> "I was able to raise $10,000. I put that into my business model funnel at the top and out of the bottom $50,000 fell out. So I'm here asking you for $10 million and the theory is that if I drop the $10 million into the top of

that funnel $50 million is going to come out.
I've proven the theory on a small scale."

That's what 99% of would-be fundraisers don't
get.

Friendly Investors 5

When you go to angel investors or venture capitalists, it's better if you've already had some people invest. Maybe not a large amount but you've found other people who thought the idea was worthwhile enough to put their money into.

These guys know very early how far you're into the game. Again:

> "Have you put up everything that you have?"

> "Yes."

Maybe that's not a lot, maybe it is. Maybe it's a great deal. Maybe it's not much. Chances are it's not a lot.

"Have you gone to talk to your mom and your dad and your aunt and your uncle and your grandmother and your grandfather?"

"Well, no. I really don't want to ask them for money."

"But you're willing to come in here and ask me for money. How come? You don't believe in it enough?"

"If I lost money it would be part of my Grandma's."

Do you see the contrast? You wouldn't believe how most people will display that. They're going to ask you questions. They are cutting questions. They are going to expose you like a gutted fish on a beach. You're going to feel pretty naked.

They're very likely to ask you if you've asked your parents, your grandparents, your aunts, your uncles, for the money.

"Well, no, I haven't really wanted to ask them for the money."

"Why?"

"I was just afraid, you know."

"But you're not afraid if you lose my money?"

See what I mean? You can really get boxed in. If you've raised some money from your parents, your friends, and your family, that's really good. We're going to go to that next but I'm not going to spend a lot of time on that because that's not going to be so much about your business place, it's not going to be so much about anything but you, your character, how much they personally believe in you, really.

The Psychology Of Persuasion

I'm going to give you a little tip for raising money from friends and family. This has really worked out well in the past. I've done it and I've seen other people do it, and it has to do with the law of consistency.

There is a guy, Robert Cialdini, a fabulous writer who has a book called *Influence: The Psychology of Persuasion*. It would be well worth reading that book before you went before any board asking for money.

Basically, people who do something once tend to do it again. One of the things that I've seen done in the past, and I've done a version of, is when you first come up with your idea and you're about to do your research it's a great idea to throw a party at your house. Have all your friends come over, have all your family come over and announce to them:

> "Hey, look, I'm starting a business. I'm in the brand new start-up stages of it and I don't know if I'm going to make any money or not but I would like to have a few thousand dollars in the bank to get started. So I have you here, my twenty best friends, my twenty closest relatives, and I'm going to ask each of you to invest $100 in my company. I'm going to keep your money in escrow; I'm not going to spend it. If I don't get this company funded within sixty days I'm going to give you your money back."

Basically they're giving you $100, right? The whole idea is that you want them to buy into your concept at the lowest amount possible that you can get them interested. At this point, with $100 they've bought into your concept.

Cialdini has this experiment that he did in this book that is just awesome. They go through a neighborhood and they ask everyone to put this giant 4'x8' sign in their front yard that said, "Slow down. Kids at Play." Only about 10% of the neighborhood agreed to put this gigantic, ugly sign in their front yard.

They then went to every other house in the neighborhood and asked them to put a little sticker in their window that said "Slow down. Children at Play" and almost everybody agreed to do that. A month later they went back to the houses that had the sticker and asked them if they could put up the sign and almost half of them agreed. It was almost a 500% increase of how many people would let them put the sign up.

Buying Into Your Concept

The bottom line was the people had bought into the concept. When they give you $100 it's no risk. If it doesn't work they'll get their money back. I would tell them:

> "If I don't get my model perfected in sixty days, I'll just give you your money back. But if I get my model perfected in sixty days I may use your money for prototyping or having a business plan writer create a business plan for me. And also, because you're investing now you'll get an opportunity to invest again before we go out to the commercial lenders."

You've already set them up so they know that if everything goes well they're going to get hit up again.

Over sixty days you can keep them updated by emails. I'd keep them on an email group list like a Yahoo! Group if you don't have anything else, or just post everything every day to a blog. Maybe you have your investor's blog, "This is what happened today. I talked to this company. I did this. Set up the business plans. Went through the projections. Here are the projections. Can anybody give me your ideas?"

Have any relatives of yours that are in business help you. They could really be a big help if you have any in your family. Almost everybody knows someone who would give them $100 to help start a business. The chances of those who gave you $100 to come back and give you $1000, or $10,000, or $20,000 is multiple-fold better because they've already gotten involved. You've had sixty days to suck them into your project. You've gotten them involved over that sixty-day period. You've given them a small piece to get involved and later on they're going to want to probably have even more involvement as they see it grow.

Think of this for a minute. You've gone through that step, and let's say you've gone back to your friends and family and raised $20,000 and that goes into your initial seed funding. When you walk into your angel investor's office, or your VC office and say:

> "Hi, my name is Perry. Here is a folder of every penny that I've put in the business. Everything that I own is in here. Here are the names and the photographs of my twenty closest relatives and friends that have together raised $22,656 because they believe in me and they believe in this project. Here is a folder with all their information in it and what they've had to say about the project."

Say to those first investors:

"I'm about to go tomorrow to get our first round of funding. Would everybody write me a single paragraph of what you think about what we're doing and what you think about our project so I can turn it in to the VC guys?"

Think of the power of that walking in versus walking in and saying, "Okay, dudes. I've got a great idea. Check it out." You're already so ahead of everybody else. It's like you walk in there wearing a Kevlar® jacket. You're bulletproof. You can still get shot down but you are so far ahead of the other guys, and with all those people behind you and all that effort behind you.

You have to remember that you're dealing with entrepreneurs. Entrepreneurs love entrepreneurs, even if they're idiot entrepreneurs. Even if they're entrepreneurs with bad ideas and misdirection they're very likely to come to you and say "Look, your thing has some hickeys on it. Here's where I see are your biggest problems. Fix these and come back and see me," if nothing else.

Do this, rather than just you walking in with a cavalier attitude and an okay idea and being overly cocky and saying, "I haven't put in any of my money. I'm not going to risk that. I have all these brains and I have all these great ideas and I'm a programmer." They're going to throw you out on your butt.

That's just a great tip for working with your friends and your family. I think it's one of the smartest things I've ever seen work in the past, is this two-step approach to raising money from your friends and family.

Demonstrate Your Character

When you go and stand in front of investors, I guess a lot of what they're looking at is your character. They know that if you've had that many people rally around you that are family and friends, those people see you as somebody that they believe in. It's twenty character witnesses with a check book.

If you have people who have given you just $100 you don't even have to particularly disclose how much a particular member gave you. You can say "These 20 people have all invested anywhere from $100 to $10,000." Tell them your lowest investor and your highest investor.

> "They invested in me because they believe in me and believe in what I'm doing, so here's what I'm bringing to the table: I'm

bringing this great idea. So far for this prototype I've proven this much of the model and I'm bringing $20,000 from them and $7000 from myself and a willingness to kill myself to make this thing work."

That is going to get you heard by very warm ears, more than anything else.

Traditional Loans 6

Loans vs. Investment

A lot of people get confused about the difference between a loan and venture capital/equity investing. If you're familiar with the financial markets, it's actually very much like stocks and bonds.

Stocks are people who are buying a piece of that company. That is what venture capital companies do, that is what angel investors do, and that is what your early stage investors do. They could loan you money, but fundamentally, most of the time, the guys like venture capital people and angel investors are equity investors. They're not loaning you money at all. They're giving you money that is not going to be paid back incrementally. It's going to be paid back when there is either a distribution of cash out of the company.

In other words, you guys are going to make a million dollars next year and everybody is going to take that million dollars out in proportion based on their ownership. This is possible, but actually most of the time they're planning on taking that money out when you sell that company, the company get acquired, or the company goes public. That's what I was talking about earlier with the liquidity event.

A loan, on the other hand, is a fixed amount of money that you borrow and pay back incrementally over a long period of time or a short period of time, depending. Some people start businesses with loans. As a matter of fact, a lot of people do. A lot of people start with the Small Business Administration.

Banks

It used to be that a lot of local banks did a lot of start-up loans many, many years ago. Due to the risk nature and all that to do with business, most banks are not entrepreneurial and they're not really business people in the normal sense of the word. The failure rate was pretty high on small business loans for banks, so most banks don't do small business loans anymore.

Banks may give you a loan and call it a "business equity lines of credit" or something like that, but basically that's an equity line on your home (or on real estate or some other asset that you own) where they'll let you borrow money for business against that house. However, they'd let you borrow money against the house to buy donuts. They don't really care that it's about business. It's just another way

of packaging a second mortgage or second
mortgage home loan.

If you have home equity it's going to be very easy
to get a business loan. You can go to your local
bank and say "I have $100,000 in home equity and
I want $50,000 to start a business." You're
probably going to walk out of there with a check.
That is one of the easiest ways. Most people freak
about putting up their home as security on a
business loan.

Community Lending Organisations

The second way that people borrow money is
through their community. Each state has some
community lending organizations. They're usually
called an Economic Development Council or
something like that at the state level. Some cities
have them where, depending upon where you're

putting your business, sometimes you can get state involvement to place a business.

I came very close to doing a deal with Arkansas Development Corporation to put a manufacturing plant in sort of a depressed area of Arkansas, a rural farm community. They were very cooperative, very easy to work with, very helpful, and they had a great deal of money available to lend. These organizations basically get block grant money and zero-interest or low-interest loan money through government programs that they then lend out to people who open businesses in minority areas and low income areas and depressed or rural areas. There are usually geographic limitations when you open your business.

A lot of people think that those programs are meant for people who live in those areas to use to open those businesses. That's not necessarily true.

Actually, the opposite could be true. You could live in Beverly Hills and still apply and get an Arkansas Community Development loan to put a manufacturing plant in Parkin, Arkansas. That's absolutely possible, and they are probably going to be more likely to give you the loan if you're an experienced businessperson and you know your trade than they are to give it to a local person who just is there and they don't particularly have skills or a plan. They have no advantage for the most part.

Like I said before, there are legal disclaimers here because I don't know if it is particularly true, but for that particular state program I don't think they have any limitations where the actual business principles have to live. It's more about where the business is placed. Many times these community loans are low interest. They have very favorable terms.

In this particular situation, they had a building they had repossessed from a loan gone bad and they were actually going to lease me the large building for $1 a year for three years if I would take it over. It was a very nice building. The deal fell apart for another reason but that's the kind of stuff that you can get a lot of times out of these organizations. They're typically lower interest loans. They're typically really easy people to work with. Just overall it's a good way to do business, and if you're opening a business that can help a community that needs it, all the better to you.

The SBA

Next is the SBA, the Small Business Administration. Historically, the SBA has been kind of hard to deal with. A lot of red tape, a lot of paperwork, a lot of crap that you had to go through just to get a loan.

Actually, the SBA doesn't make any loans. Participating banks make loans for the SBA. The bank makes the loan but the loan is guaranteed by the Small Business Administration. With these what takes so much time is all this documentation that has to go through the SBA. Everything to do with your business and everything to do with you: your capitalization, your business plans, your cash flow projections. It's just a huge amount of paperwork.

If you decide to go that route you'd better find somebody that has prepared those documents before and is an expert at preparing SBA loan documents. I would strongly suggest that you go that route but it's probably going to take you anywhere between three and five months to get funded if you do.

Your Capacity

They're going to look for four criteria in dealing with you. Number one is capacity: the ability for you to repay the loan. That is the first thing they're going to look at. Does this person have a viable business model that shows enough cash flow and enough projected profit to realistically make these loan payments?

You have to know exactly how to talk to both kinds of organization. A lending organization and an angel investor firm are completely different. When dealing with a lending organization like the SBA, you need to be conservative in your estimates. They want to be assured that you're going to make enough profit to pay them. That's their number one concern. They don't care how much your company is going to be worth. They don't care about your future valuation. They don't care about how much you'll be able to sell out for and make billions of dollars. They don't care about any of that. They care that you're going to make enough money consistently in your business to be able to make your note payment every month. That is their number one criteria. If you project too high in your projections to the SBA you might blow them out of the water because they're going to look at it and say it's not realistic and that this person is a pipe dreamer.

Your Capital Assets

Second, they're going to look at your capital assets. What are you putting up, in an SBA loan situation, in collateral for the loan? They have various requirements and it varies, but they're going to want to know, "What if this goes south? What if you borrow this money from us and can't pay it? What is our salvage value? What can we probably get out of here with?"

The more solid assets you are buying, the better off you'll be. For instance, the SBA is a great place to go if you're going to build a car wash and 90% of your investment is land and equipment. If you're going to buy an existing business the SBA is a fabulous opportunity. The SBA is fabulous for working with franchise companies, and most franchise companies have professionals in their home offices that will actually work on these SBA applications with you and have a really great working knowledge of the SBA.

These guys are a lot more conservative in what they're looking for, and they love franchises. About 60% of all start-up businesses fail within the first five years. Only about 15% of franchise opportunities fail within the first five years. The

SBA knows the success rate of most of these franchises is relatively high.

Conditions Of The Market

They're also going to look at the conditions of your market. What's surrounding you? What influences your business? Are there market fluctuations? Are you in a seasonal business where you're going to have a difficult time paying in the summer or the winter? Do political things such as currency rates change how your business operates?

Unlike a venture capitalist that is going to invest money in your business and not going to look for a monthly return, the SBA is only concerned whether or not you're going to have consistent cash flow to make your payment every month. That is their number one concern.

They're going to look at the conditions of your business. What is there about it that could potentially be risky? What could change your business model? Do you only have one customer? Or do you have a number of customers? Customer lists are a big deal.

Your Character

Finally, and very important, is your character. They're going to look at the character of the person that they're dealing with. Have you been in a lot of legal trouble in the past? Have you had good credit history in the past? Do you tend to be a person who pays their bills and obligations? I can't give you the exact credit score that they're looking for but I've heard that the minimum credit score is around 680. You may have to have some character witnesses and some other things to come forth on your behalf to accomplish getting an SBA loan.

Funding Timescale

All that being said, you have to have all of that together, all of you paperwork together, and you have about anywhere from a three to five month wait.

They say that if you used the Preferred Lender Network, the PLN, that you could probably get your loan through in as little as six to eight weeks. That is just about as good as it gets. That is from the day that you have the package completely prepared.

Putting Together The Package

The package is going to be daunting to you, especially if you don't have very good accounting skills. Most of it is not fill-in-the-blank forms. A lot of it is attaching spreadsheets or PNLs or all these things that you might not understand.

Much of it comes down to projections. The SBA is going to ask you for projections: projecting out what you think you're going to make in a year, three years, five years, or whatever. I would project on the conservative side. Make sure your numbers make a reasonable profit, a fair profit; but I would definitely project on the conservative side when dealing with a lending institution like the Small Business Administration.

The SBA Express Loan

Now, let me tell you about the hot, good, super-cool news that nobody else is probably telling you about the SBA. The SBA has a number of brand new programs right now. The one that is getting the most buzz is not necessarily the most important one, but I'm going to tell you about it anyway. It's called the SBA Express Loan.

What that means is that the SBA has come up with a program that started out at $150,000 and now this program is up to $350,000. You can actually go to an SBA lender bank, or partner bank, and borrow up to $350,000 from the SBA. Fill out your paperwork on a very short application, which is usually one that comes from the actual bank itself because they're letting the bank make the credit decision and gather all the financial data. I don't even know if they actually see the financial data. They're taking the bank's word for it. The reason that they are taking the bank's word for it is that instead of guaranteeing 75% or 85% of the loan, they only guarantee 50% of the loan on an SBA Express Loan.

Here's what the lender is going to be looking for: hard assets of at least 50% of what you want to borrow. In other words, you either need to have hard assets that you already own that you're willing to pledge (which you probably don't want to do) or secondly, you need to be buying hard assets.

This is a great loan program. For instance, if you're starting a street sweeper business and you need to buy two street sweepers and you need $200,000 to buy those sweepers that are $75,000 each and $50,000 to operate for the first six months until you start making a profit, then that would be a very viable candidate for this loan. The bank is going to look at it and say, "Okay, they're putting up assets of more than 50%, and the SBA is guaranteeing the other 50% so the bank has very limited risk."

There is a downside about an Express Loan. A bank can charge up to 6.5% over prime rate for a loan up to $50,000, and up to 4.5% over prime rate for anything over $50,000 so this is probably going to be pretty expensive money. You can shop the rate. It doesn't mean they have to charge the maximum but a lot of banks do charge maximum. The really cool news is that you will get an answer within 36 hours of filing your application. So, literally, if you file your application on a Wednesday, on Friday the banker is going to call you and tell you if you got the money or not. Obviously, if someone's looking to get cash fast this would be a viable way to go. It's an up or down answer. You have to have decent credit, you have to have collateral to back the loan, and you have to have a viable business plan to show your banker who is probably not going to care about it a lot.

They're going to be more concerned with the equity that you have. What do you have to put up? Or what are you going to do with the money? They're not going to just give you the money and just hope that you go buy these hard assets.

They're going to say, "Go buy the bulldozer and we'll send the check to the bulldozer company." They're going to hold the title on the bulldozer. They want to make sure they have their security net.

The SBA Community Express Loan

There are two more areas that SBA has done an Express Program and they're really, really interesting if you're in a particular situation. One is called the SBA Community Express Loan Package. With Community Express it's like the Express Package but just a little bit different. With the Community Express Package the maximum is $250,000. Here's the good news: they follow the standard SBA guarantee percentage line, which is usually 75-85% of the loan.

Say you're in a business where it's $200,000 – you need to buy $50,000 worth of equipment, and you need $150,000 in working capital – this is a line that may work for you. It allows revolving loans for up to seven years. The interest rates are the same as a normal SBA loan. Most of this is the same as a normal SBA loan. What makes it different is that the lenders are not required to take collateral for up to $25,000 loan. If you want a small loan you can get it, if the banker is willing to give it to you, without any collateral and still have a guarantee from the SBA. They normally require the banks to hold some collateral so you have skin in the game.

The trick here is that these loans are only available to businesses that they are going to place in particular communities. This is another geographically targeted program. Don't discount that right away. You'd be surprised at how many areas are available for this kind of lending. It's not nearly as tight as the community development areas. A lot of fringe areas are going to be available through this program. It's a good program overall and it's a great way to get most of your loan guaranteed through SBA by just picking a place that you're going to put your business that is advantageous.

There may be some banks that require some employment requirements like "How many people are you going to employ?" and stuff like that. Some of the community development loans are like that. They're trying to incentivize people to go in and stimulate growth in some of these areas.

The SBA Patriot Express Pilot Loan Incentive

The program that I think is probably one of the most exciting programs is going to only apply to a certain amount of people that read this, but you may know somebody that you can work with. It's called the Patriot Express Pilot Loan Incentive.

They have an awesome program now at SBA. It's $500,000 and it runs the same terms as the normal SBA Express Loan except they guarantee 75-85% of the loan, which is a huge amount. If you're borrowing $200,000 you're only going to have to collateralize about $30-50,000 of it. The rate is crazy, crazy cheap compared to the other SBA loans. The maximum they can charge is 2.25% over prime for the first seven years and 2.75% over prime for anything longer than seven years.

The eligibility requirement, the reason they call it the Patriot Express Program, is it's only available to certain people: veterans who have been honorably discharged (or not dishonorably discharged); active duty military personnel; retirees within 24 months of separation from active duty or within 12 months of discharge; Reservists and National Guard members; and spouses of all of the above. If you're a spouse or a widow of a military person you have the ability to borrow $500,000 from the SBA at a very high guaranteed rate with a very low interest rate.

Again, these are streamlined forms that are super easy to fill out. They'll work with you and there are even some agencies out there right now that are helping some of the military widows walk through the process, or some of the military guys who are coming back from military action right now and finding out they don't have a job because they've been gone for so long.

This is an awesome program for people who want to come back and start a business, and the really cool part? It's a 36-hour approval process for up to $500,000, 75-85% guaranteed. This initial loan is up to seven years and it can have maturity extensions outside that.

Even if you're deployed, your spouse could do it. It's actually kind of built for that. Your wife could do all of the documentation here on this side and actually could start a business that you could have when you get back.

It's really an awesome program for the people it applies to. It's just an absolutely fabulous program.

SBA Micro-Loans

Also, SBA has a low dock program that is for smaller loans. They have a micro-loan program. The low dock program is basically very much like the Express program for smaller loans. It has a one-page application and it gets approval in 36 hours. Most people use that for loans of $50,000 or so if they just want a small, small business loan.

It's almost like getting an SBA credit card. If you can apply for a high-limit credit card and get it, you can probably get that loan from SBA or from your local bank with SBA. You really don't have to have a business plan or any of that stuff to go with it. They're just basically giving you a personal credit line of $50,000 if you have decent credit.

It's not nearly as daunting as going in front of venture capitalists, but you have to make sure. $50,000 for people who have never been in business sounds like a whole lot of money. For a guy like me who is already in business, $50,000 is two weeks payroll. It can go really fast depending on what you're doing.

SBA Micro-Lending Community Programs

Lastly they have a micro lending program that's available through some of the community lending organizations. If you look up SBA micro lending online you'll get all the information that you want. I doubt that very many people reading would be greatly interested in it but if you are by all means look it up.

Mainly it gives loans from $1000-25,000 and it's usually for those on a very low income: former welfare recipients; people with physical disabilities; those living in super-low income areas; and other low income individuals who want to start a business to better their life. However, it maxes out at about $25,000.

It's a pretty simple process and you don't have to have a very high credit requirement to get it either. It's not really judged on credit but more on your ability to participate in some of their training programs and some other things. If you're willing to participate in a lot of programs and learn more about business and how you can make a living on your own, the SBA will work with you and train you. If you complete all the steps that they want they will actually loan you a small amount of seed money to start a business. It's a pretty cool program.

Other SBA Resources

The SBA has come a long way. I really used to discourage people away from them. Not anymore. The SBA has come a long way in the last few years, making the process much more reasonable to go with.

Anyone interested in learning more about the SBA should go to www.SBA.gov. In fact, I would suggest that to anybody. I don't care if you're going to go to venture capitalists or what; they have some of the best business planning tools that you'll find anywhere, such as business form templates and entrepreneurial start-ups and things like that. These things will get you to understand what is going to be required of you starting a business. They have tons of planners for how to plan a business, start it, and how manage it once it's open.

A lot of entrepreneurs, and I'm including myself in this, just suck at management. Even if you're terrible at management, chances are you're not going to be able to hire a great manager right at first so you're going to have to learn to manage it while you get by.

They also have a lot of good information on compliance and regulations for businesses, a lot of online training, a lot of video training, PowerPoint training. They have some information about grants and even disaster assistance stuff. The SBA does a lot of lending to those who have been in a disaster, like Hurricane Katrina, for instance. They lent money to businesses to rebuild after disasters. That's pretty common.

I don't think they actually do grants. They help people to get grants but they don't actually do grants directly. They have some marketing training, although it's probably pretty weak coming from the government. They'll even show you their district offices where you can go and actually talk to them.

Their SCORE is an awesome program. They have small business development centers across the country too where you can get a lot of resources. I know many people who have found angel investors through SCORE. It's a program put on by the SBA and it's basically retired entrepreneurs and retired business people who volunteer at the SBA to help young entrepreneurs. You can't buy that kind of advice.

You can call them up and make an appointment and go out and meet with them, or they'll come out and meet with you at your business. Usually they are people who have volunteered to work with entrepreneurs. Sort of like if you volunteer to work with puppy dogs. These are people who just absolutely love entrepreneurs. They tend to find themselves getting involved. They'll start out as just a mentor but a lot of times these people will get involved. Just the connections that they can give you to the go-to guys can be priceless. It's a free service to you that probably 99% of start-ups don't take advantage of.

They have a SCORE blog just for women's businesses. They've really gotten deeply involved. SCORE works with American Express a lot as well. There are just all kinds of resources there for you and I really suggest you take a look. They are at www.SCORE.org. They're not a government agency but a non-profit organization that happens to partner with the SBA.

Angel Investors   7

An angel investor is really a very simple concept.
Angel investors are a lot like venture capitalists. I
get excited about angel investors because I think
it's one of the best places for people that do have a
good plan to become funded. If you're going to go
out for funding, I'd definitely go to angel groups or
angel investors before you go to venture
capitalists.

An angel investor is somebody that invests in high-
risk business ventures and start-up ventures in the
really early stages. They usually invest somewhere
between $25,000 and $2 million. $2 million in the
angel deals are really big angel investors. You
don't see a lot of those, but they happen.

Believing In You

There's a big difference between an angel investor and a venture capital company: they're investing their own money. I can't emphasize how important that really is. If they have the actual belief in you when they get on your bandwagon, if they drink your Kool-Aid, as we say, they have the ability to sit down this afternoon and stroke you a check. They're not bound by any particular fiduciary responsibilities other than their own. They're only risking their money, so they don't have to jump through a lot of hoops, they don't have to go to a lot of boards. It's basically like that old movie, *Wall Street*. Gordon Gecko wrote Bud a million-dollar check and delivered it to him the next morning in his office. An angel investor can do that if they totally believe in what you're doing.

They're pretty smart people, so they're typically not really impulsive people. They do make decisions quickly. It's a much faster process. That's a big advantage to using an angel investor: you can usually get your funding done a lot quicker, you can actually get the money in the bank a whole lot quicker, and overall it's a better solution than going to venture capitalists on the front end, for sure.

The other thing is that if you're going to raise some seed money, and you're not going to have to give up a whole lot of your company to do it, almost all angel investors have relationships with venture capitalists. So if you're in the start-up stages and you can bring in an angel investor to help you, they're going to be able to walk over with you, introduce you to a venture capitalist and say "Hey, we have this great deal and you should probably listen." It's a thousand times better than you walking in off the street and pitching your deal to a VC firm.

High Returns

There aren't a great deal of negatives if you understand that these are people who are clearly looking to make high returns on their investment. They can already make modest returns, maybe 10% returns or more in stock markets, bond markets, commodities, things like that, so they're not going to be interested in earning 10% or even 20% or 30% returns on their money. They're interested in investing start-up companies and earning three to ten times their initial investment in a period of maybe 18 to 24 months.

Maybe you're thinking, "Oh, man, that's just ridiculous, they want that much more money back!" The reason they want that much money back is because an angel investor is more likely to invest in an idea or a really premature-level business than a venture capital company is, and when you're investing in that sort of stuff, you have a lot of failures. So on the winners they make three to ten times, and on the losers they lose 100%.

The good news is, if you pick more winners than losers in that business, you make a lot of money as far as angel investors go. I like it. It's a good path.

Getting An Angel Investor

Say you have a great idea and a great concept, you've proven some of your concept, and you really know your industry. If you have some leverage to work from – you went through the first two steps of this process and you put all your skin on the table, you got people involved, you really put together a comprehensive plan, you know your industry, you know your market, you really feel what you're doing is going to be successful – then you're going to be able to go out and choose an angel investor.

Like I said before, there's way more money out there than are good deals. That's just an absolute fact. People believe that it's a one in a million shot if they get funded. That's just not true. If you have everything it takes, you can get funded right away.

I watched Pamela Anderson on the Jay Leno show not too long ago, and she was in Hollywood for two weeks before she got her first national TV series. She had everything that she needed. You can think about that any way you want to. She was the full package, and she was able to get placed really quickly. So would you if you have a good, solid opportunity.

So here's what you want to do: you want to put them on an interview almost as much as they're interviewing you. In your angel partners you should look for people who have business knowledge. I don't like dealing with angels that have just come from the finance world. There are a lot of those out there, guys that have been Wall Street guys or finance guys. I prefer to try finding angel investors that are in the stratosphere of business that I'm operating in.

Industry Experts

If you're in the tech business, there are a ton of them. In New York, Austin, LA, Bay Area for sure, and the Silicon Valley area, there are tons of investors. In any industry that's typically on the rise you're going find a good number of angel investors. You want to make sure that they have general business knowledge and understand how a business operates day to day and not from some giant corporate level. I like for them to have industry expertise.

Somebody that knows my industry is so much easier to work with, and they're going to offer a lot. There's the concept of smart money and dumb money. What you want to raise is smart money, which is money that comes with experience. The knowledge of people who are a lot smarter than you are can direct you. What an angel investor really would like to do is to find a subject that they can coach really well without a whole lot of time, that will listen, pay attention to what they have to say. They don't want to run your company, but they would certainly like for you to be a good coaching client.

Contacts

The biggest thing your angel can give you is contacts. This can be worth more than anything.

A lot of times, a great place to find an angel investor is with people who have been involved in a publicly traded company in your industry, like a founder of a publicly traded company that was acquired by somebody else and they were no longer needed. They have $20-$30 million sitting around and they know your industry upside-down and backwards.

They're not really interested in going out and starting another business because it's just too much work. Once you get past a certain age, you're going to find out that starting a new business is not as appealing to you as it used to be, especially if you're sitting on a big bag full of money. Getting to use their knowledge as a springboard would be a really great thing to have.

For them, it means they can spread their knowledge around. If they can give four or five different companies in the industry a couple hundred thousand dollars apiece, it's no real money out of their pocket, but they get involved in it.

Their contacts are gigantic. One of my first mentors was a man named Kimmons Wilson, the founder of Holiday Inns. I met him by total accident. I called to buy a piece of equipment from a friend of mine one day. It was in a building that I'd seen that he was leasing. He said "Well, that's not mine. That's Mr. Wilson's piece of equipment." I had a manufacturing company then. I said "Do you have a phone number for this Mr. Wilson?" I had no idea who he was. I called him up and his secretary put my right through to him without screening the call or anything.

He was in his eighties at that time. I asked him if he wanted to sell that piece of equipment and he started asking me "What are you going to do with it? What kind of business do you have?" There was a point in the call that I just wanted to say "Man, do you want to sell the piece of equipment or not? I don't really have a lot of time to screw around." But for whatever reason, something told me not to do that. I explained to him my entire business, what I was doing, and he said, "Well, come down here and let's ride down and take a look at the piece of equipment."

This was a piece of equipment that I think I wanted to buy for $1,000. I didn't know who this guy was at the time. I said okay, I hung up the phone and the guy that was sitting across from me said, "Who was that?" I said, "That was some older guy that's got a piece of equipment. He's really weird, asking me a lot of questions and wants me to come get him to go see it." He said, "What's his name?" "Kimmons Wilson."

The guy's eyes got big and he said "Man, don't you know who that is?" I was living in Memphis, Tennessee at the time. He said "That's the founder of Holiday Inns, Wilson World Hotels." He was also the first guy who sold popcorn in a movie theatre. He owned all the Wurlitzer jukeboxes in the entire south United States, he founded Holiday Inns, and later in life he invented the timeshare. So he did a few things.

He was an absolutely accomplished guy that had multiple hotel holdings and all that. He'd sold out of Holiday Inn, but the bottom line was he loved entrepreneurs. I was probably the first entrepreneur that had picked up the phone and called him in God knows when. He was interested in what I was doing and went on to become a great mentor to me. We never actually got in a business venture together. He was an investor and I didn't need an investor at the time.

Sometimes I would call Kimmons and say "Man, I'm having a real hard time trying to find this or trying to get this or that done," and he could pick up the phone and call the president of the bank or the mayor or whomever and say "Hey, I have this guy, and he's having a real hard time. Can you help him out?" "Oh sure, Mr. Wilson, no problem!" It was just like I walked in the door. That was incredibly important. You're going to find that these angel investors are those kinds of people.

Support

Hopefully you're going to find an angel investor that's supportive, too. Along the way you're going to get your brains kicked in every now and then. You almost need somebody that's been there and done that who can go:

> "Man, it's not the end of the world. It's going to be fine. Don't worry about it. Let's just regroup tomorrow and figure out what we're going to do to overcome this thing."

That makes a giant difference in how well you do.

Follow-Up Financing

Lastly, just like we talked about before with the $100 investor party, angel investors are going to be your first line of follow-up financing. If an angel investor gives you $50,000 in seed money to get your venture off the ground, when it's really successful and you need $500,000 or $1 million to do your deal to get it to national level, it's very likely that your first angel investor may be willing to come up with that additional funding.

They're going to know you intimately by this point. They're going to know your business model intimately. They're going to know your product. They're very likely to have other friends that are willing to come in, other angel investors that may be willing to come in. You don't have to go out to the venture capital firms.

What Motivates Angel Investors?

This is something that almost everybody gets wrong, and it's a big point. Angel investors are motivated by profit. There's no question of that. But that is way down on the list of why angel investors are involved in angel investing.
The number one reason, far and above everything else is the thrill of entrepreneurship. Why is that

important to them? An entrepreneur is an entrepreneur, I think. I think you're almost born with it. If you are reading this right now, you are probably born with that itchy gene that digs in your gut every morning when you wake up that makes you want to do more in life. You're constantly pursuing excellence and wanting to always doing better today than you were doing yesterday.

I hate New Year's. I don't think I've ever had a happy New Year. I sit around and evaluate my previous year and all I could have done better and how much more productive I could have been and how far away I am from these final goals, things like that.

If you're a person that re-evaluates, you're probably a born entrepreneur. Almost all angel investors are born entrepreneurs. They love nothing more than hanging out with other entrepreneurs. They don't necessarily like running businesses. They have been in a business, gotten in it, made their money, and gotten out. They're not terribly interested in running a business.

Most entrepreneurs detest running a business. They love starting businesses. The start-up is the fun part. It's the hardest part, but it's also the most fun and challenging part of business. Once you've done it a few times, you're good at it, you have a talent for it, and it's almost like being a great singer. Most great singers would tell you they'd go out and sing for free if they couldn't get paid. Angel investors are the same way. They just want to be involved in the entrepreneurial cycle. They want to vicariously live through the other entrepreneurs. They don't necessarily want to jump out there, roll their sleeves up, and work the 14-hour days that they used to when they were younger. It's a great partnership! You get to use their knowledge and their money, they get to use your fresh ideas and your boundless energy. And they provide the wisdom and the know-how and the experience.

Knowing that, know this: there are two things that angel investors are going to really look for:

1: How exciting is what you're doing? If you're going into the port-a-potty business, you have to figure out a way to make the port-a-potty business sound cool, sound sexy, which isn't always the easiest thing in the world to do!

2: How high is your energy level? That's the thing they probably need more than they need anything: your energy and your wide-eyed optimism. They know that they don't have that. They like to see a lack of any fear because they've had their teeth kicked in enough that they're fearful. Smart investors see that.

Ignorance Of Fear

It's like you see these crazy guys do this motocross jumping. You see these guys out there that are turning upside-down and doing cartwheels and crap on a motorcycle jumping two big humps of dirt. Not a lot of fifty-year-olds out there doing that.

It's not that there aren't fifty-year-old guys out there who are physically fit enough. There are guys out there that are plenty physically fit and have the physical capability to do it. They're in better shape than some of the guys that are on the motorcycles. But they lack the benefit of ignorance.

There's sort of a benefit to being ignorant. My first business was that I built 42 jewelry stores when I was 19 years old. I opened 42 jewelry stores in 18 months, and I think I did it just because nobody told me you couldn't do that. Today, if somebody came to me and said "Hey, got a great idea. We're going to open 42 jewelry stores in 18 months," I'd tell them they were out of their mind, it can't be done.

The young entrepreneur energetic mind can do things that are Olympic. You don't see old guys at the Olympics, even though they're fit. You start believing less of what you can do as you get older.

Learn From Their Mistakes

Now, these angel investors, they see your excitement and your idea and the lack of fear, and to some extent they will protect you from failure so you keep that, especially if they have a vested interest. What they're not going to tolerate is you continually ignoring their advice:

"Look, I know where you're going and I understand why you're going there. Let me tell you, every time I've ever tried that in the past, that's dead-ended into a brick wall. You're probably going to hit a brick wall."

If you do this, you're going to end up in some sort of adversarial relationship. You need to take to heart that they have been there and done that.
I had a deal not too long ago where I was dealing with a company and the founder of the company kept continually wanting to sell what people needed, not what they wanted. We went round and round and round about it. I know, from my experience, people buy way more of what they want than what they need. That concept wouldn't sink in. As it turned out, I passed the deal onto somebody else. It didn't work out for us, and long-term, I don't believe it'll work out for him, either.

Letting You Fail

Having said this, they certainly don't want you calling them for every decision. It's the last thing in the world they want. If they have to run the company, they'll just go run them a company and make all the money. They don't want that. They want you to go out and run it. Yeah, they're going to hold you accountable when you make mistakes.

Most of them are not just going to bust your balls super-hard because you screwed up and did something wrong. A lot of times they're just going to chuckle about it and go "Yeah, I could have told you it was going to happen if you had asked. That's okay. You need to learn." That is, if it's not a massive, catastrophic disaster.

They'll tolerate mistakes. They don't want to break your spirit. They know that the entrepreneur's spirit is what's profitable for them, so they don't want to break your spirit. That's the last thing in the world they want to do.

Nice Guy Investors

A lot of angel investors, I call them "nice guy investors," are just wanting to invest in their community. You see a lot of this in inner-city ethnic communities, poor communities, small towns, rural areas, that local boy done good, comes back home and helps fledgling entrepreneurs to support the community from a little town. There are a lot of great stories of inner-cities.

I can't remember his name right now, but there's an angel investor that owned tons of inner-city food franchises, Wendy's and all that. He made millions, and now he goes back and angel-invests in super-poor, inner-city areas. It's very rewarding for him. He's basically angel-investing for emotional reward. You're going to find people that do that. Don't believe that that's the motivation for most angel investors. But there are some of them.

Balancing Their Portfolio

A lot of them are people who are balancing their portfolio. If they read enough investment books, it's going to tell them to take one 1% or 2% of their total portfolio (if they have a lot of money) and invest it in angel investing. As a matter of fact, my broker by Merrill-Lynch handles all major stuff. He's a major wealth management guy. One of the things that they tell all their people who have larger accounts is, "Take 3% or 4% of your portfolio and invest it in something you find fun. Leave the other 97% to us and we'll go make you money."

Find something that you enjoy, that's fun to you. It kind of keeps you out of screwing around with all their real investment decisions that they should be making. They know if you're not occupied with that 2% or 3% that you have, then you're going to want to screw around with the two or three or ten million that you have in your account and try to become an armchair stockbroker, which is, by the way, a pretty bad idea.

For the most part, unless you're just really skilled, the wealth management people are so much more. When you get to that point, you have plenty of money so find yourself a really good wealth manager. You talk about the Holy Grail of where to find angel investors – that's where you find them. My broker brings me deals from time to time, people he meets and things like that. Brokers are really reluctant to do that, because if I get a bad deal, they're afraid it might reflect on the broker, so you have to put that broker at ease.

Staying Involved In Business

Another reason for angel investors is that they
want to keep engaged. They want to keep working,
be involved because they know that they've seen
their buddies retire and a year later they've died
because they were just bored out of their brains.

I've had three or four guys back when I was still
doing consulting work who actually said that's
why they were still working. I was sitting across
from a wealthy man who was in his eighties and I
said, "Why are you still doing this?" He said, "I
don't want to die." There's a guy in our building
that's running a company right now, and he said
that he came out of retirement for his fourth time
to come in.

A lot of these guys do that to keep involved, keep
active, keep their minds sharp. If you're out of

business for very long, you really lose touch. Most of these angel investors, they just don't want to lose touch with what's going on. That's the reason they really like investing in the new, the exciting, newer generation, younger stuff because it keeps them in connection with what's going on.

They love problem-solving. They want to show off their expertise just like anybody does. If you're a great pianist, you want to play the piano for people. That's what you want to do. Most of the time, the funny part about entrepreneurs is that they're all- encompassed in their entrepreneurship. A lot of them don't have a lot of other interests. Their real hobby is how to make money. It's their identity. It's what they do. I know tons and tons of guys just like me that read The Wall Street Journal for fun. Most people would just rather take a beating.

There are some funny entrepreneur tests, like if you go to Office Depot more than you go to the grocery store, you could be an entrepreneur. A lot of guys are entrepreneurs, especially guys who are angel investors. They're absorbed in business. They're totally absorbed in it, which makes them great at it. But they're just like a fanatic in any other way. My neighbor across the street is a bicycle fanatic. His whole family bicycles in the morning, they bicycle in the afternoon, and he has bicycle racks on all his cars. He's a cyclist. That's what he does. Every spare moment, he's cycling. Every spare moment, I'm an entrepreneur. A lot of people are like that.

Finding Your Angel Investor 8

Now we're going to move over to the area that you've wanted to get to for so long: where you can find a guy like Kimmons Wilson; where to get your own angel investor.

Networking

A lot of the time you'll stumble across them by being exposed a lot. Sitting in your office all day, not making business contacts, is not the way to do it.

Networking is probably one of the hardest things. I've always had a hard time with networking, and it's one of the hardest things to understand for a lot of people, particularly people who are not necessarily social. How do you move into warm situations and get to know people?

You want to come up with an affinity group first. Make a list of people that you know already who may know other people. Make a list of people that you would like to know, your hit list, your target list, your dream list. I'd love to have lunch with Trump, you know. Put it on your list, it doesn't matter. They say there's only six degrees of separation between everybody on the planet, so aim high. Why not?

You'd be surprised at how easy it is to get to people, particularly in your local market that are considered locally famous. It's relatively easy to get to them. They know a lot of people in local markets, people like soccer coaches and golf buddies. People have recreational friends, and you may play golf with a guy that plays golf with the mayor.

Depending on whom you're trying to get to know or who you're trying to get to, that's one way. Make a list of your friends first. Put a star by the ones that you think may know people of influence. Or people who are of high net worth or may be interested in entrepreneurial endeavors.

Business Brokers

One of my secret honey holes of people is business brokers. Business brokers are some of the best people you can know but they get a constant stream of people, and probably 75% of business broker clients are people who are looking to start businesses or buy a business that's already in existence because they've sold another business or exited out of another company. They've probably got the direct line, direct hook-up.

The problem is they're trying to sell them business because they want to make a big $40,000, $50,000 payday. What you can do is a technique called "bird doggie" – go to those business broker guys and say "Hey, if you find me a guy, I have stock for you. I'll give you a piece of the deal or some of my seed money." If you've raised $20,000 from your friends and neighbors, agree to give that guy $5,000 and some stock if he'll help you find an angel investor or make an introduction for you. They're going to have a ton of those people that they meet.

The funny part about business brokers is that most of the people calling to buy a business never do. The reason they don't is because when they go into businesses, the businesses are screwed up or something is wrong with them or whatever. The idea of it is really cool, and then when they get into it, the thought of having to come in every day and fix problems and get back into delving into the management of the company again is not as exciting as it was in concept. The reality is just not as cool.

They're a prime candidate to fund a start-up. They get all the excitement and involvement they want without any of the management. Management is like kryptonite to entrepreneurs. We hate it. We will run from it at every possible opportunity. When you show us a company that's for sale and you say, "Oh, yeah, it's a great company, great idea, great product, they just have some management problems," we go "AHH!!"

Almost all companies that are for sale have some management problems because they were started by whom? Entrepreneurs that didn't manage! Business brokers will tell you the best buyers they ever find for businesses are management people that have come out of corporations with a package and have money. They'll go "Oh, that company

just needs to be managed. Okay, I'll go manage it."
They make great buyers, they run the companies,
they're successful, and yada, yada, yada.

Target The Right People

I have a rule of networking: only target the people
you want. Seems basic. But what people tend to do
in networking is they tend to go out and network
with their peers because they feel comfortable, that
they'll be accepted. You should really be trying to
network with people at least one step above you in
the evolutionary chain.

If you're trying to get somewhere, network with
people who are already where you're trying to get.
Most people will tend to try to network with
people on the same level as them because it's
comfortable. It's easier, and they'll talk to them.
It's really a lateral move. You're not really moving

up the ladder any when you do that. They may know some people you can move up the ladder through, but then you kind of feel like you're using them or whatever. So you need to stretch yourself a little bit and get out there.

What Can You Do For Them?

A guy was telling me a great story not too long ago. This fellow became a best selling author. He has a lot of books. He wrote a book in its entirety that he thought Jay Conrad Levinson's audience would appreciate. He thought that Levinson's audience would buy it, and it was an extension for his guerrilla marketing business. He wrote the book and sent it to him and said, "I want to give you this book. Go sell it as yours. I've ghost-written it for you. Just add me as a co-author, and that'd be super. You keep all the money."

He spent a year writing a book and gave it away. There's no real downside to that whatsoever for Levinson. He sold the book, it's very popular, and the co-author's popular. Now the co-author got a publishing deal to do a next book, which was his book, and it's very successful. Now he does a series of books and speaking engagements and a lot of other things. He's doing really, really well. He gave something at first.

The problem is that most people call in favors or try to network with people and say, "What can you do for me?" Your approach needs to be "What can I do for you?" A lot of times, do it without asking. If it can cause no harm to them, like the book, just do it without asking.

I worked with a guy twenty years ago in the insurance business who was insanely successful as a life insurance agent. He did it at first, himself, and then eventually he had his secretary do it.

Every week, he would clip out a newspaper clipping. Most newspapers show promotions, and he would clip out a newspaper clipping of "Jimmy was promoted to this" or whatever. They would photocopy it and he would laminate the copy and send it with a letter of congratulations to the person who got promoted in the local community:

> "Hey, saw that you were promoted! Congratulations on your success. It's people like you that drive our community, blah, blah, blah, sincerely, John Smith."

Don't try to sell them something. Don't try to ask for anything right then. It needs to be genuine interest. Just say "Hey, man, I'm glad for you. I'm happy for you." The fact that you took the time to clip that thing, laminate that thing, mail it to them, it's a big deal!

Back to Robert Cialdini's book, it's called An Obligatory Base. Cialdini did an experiment where I think they had two monkeys paint these pictures. There was no artistic value to these two paintings. They gave people this test. They said:

> "Hey, you want a certificate for a $1,000 painting, you can take your $1,000 certificate, you walk into a room, there are two paintings, and you choose which one you want. You get it and you get to go home with it."

It's worth $1,000, supposedly. They brought all these people in, and in an experiment they had two different people stand by the paintings like they were the artists. Roughly half the people bought the painting on the left and half the people bought the painting on the right. In a further experiment they started having one of the artists walk out and go get a Coke. He would come back in the room and he'd say "Hey, I went to go get myself a Coke and I brought you one. Here you go." Then both of the artists would leave the room again. The paradigm shifted. Almost 80% of the people bought the painting from the guy who brought them a Coke.

There is an obligatory base there and there's a reciprocal need. As humans, we feel the need to reciprocate. Particularly, it's easy to reciprocate. We want to. We have an obligation. It's a monkey on our back if we don't reciprocate. The easiest way to reciprocate is to recommend. You'll find that when you do that, a large percentage of people will give you a call or drop you an e-mail and say "Hey, I just wanted to say thanks, blah, blah, blah, if there's anything I could ever do for you, just let me know."

You don't necessarily want to fire them back an e-mail and say "Oh, by the way, here's something you can do for me right now!" The point is, if you do that for a little while, when you go out to some of the functions and the chamber events and things we're going to talk about in a few minutes, and you have your name tag on, you're not going to be the Lone Ranger anymore. You're not going to be the only guy there. You're going to know somebody. People are going to come up and go:

> "Hey! You're Perry! I got your thing in the mail and I just want to say thank you over some cocktails. What do you do?"

They become interested in you.

> "Right now I'm involved in a start-up, I'm doing this, this, and this. We're in our funding stage."

I want you to write this down and never forget it:

"Oh, by the way, do you know anybody that has been involved in this industry or has just retired that might be willing to sit down and give me some advice about my start-up?"

Don't say, "Do you know anybody that has a checkbook?" Say, "Do you know anybody that might be willing to sit down and give me some advice?"

That's a big, big, big secret. Most people do, and most people are willing to give advice.

Gather Introductions

One of the biggest things that you need is introductions. It's funny, my buddies and I used to go out to bars, and believe me, I used to be quite the "lady-killer." We had this whole group of guys, and one of the biggest tricks that we found was if one of us wanted to meet a girl, we would have the other one go over and get the girl, bring her over and introduce her to us. She didn't know the person introducing, but the approach was so good, it worked so much better than walking up and saying, "Hi, my name is Perry. How are you?"

It's better off to have my buddy come over and say, "Hey, come here for a minute," and just ask her to walk over across the bar. "I want you to meet my friend Perry. What's your name, honey?" "Lisa." "Hi, Lisa. This is my friend Perry. I just wanted to introduce you to him." "Oh, hi, Perry. How are you doing?" Then the conversation starts. It works three or four times as well as just a normal conversation.

The same is going to be true when you're meeting your angel investor. If you're sitting down with that angel investor because of a blind e-mail or because he saw your business plan posted on the

Internet or whatever, he's got big giant question marks going off in his head. His radar is going off, his guard is up big time, he doesn't know you from Adam, and as far as he knows, you're just a swindler trying to get money out of him.

You're setting things up as far as your network, you almost make it to where you're just there and they become interested in you. Then it's more of them pursuing you than you pursuing them.

Let's reverse for a minute and go back into where we were raising our groups of our 20 friends to come to our party and give us $100. Those people will become hyper-referrers for you. Be sure to really think about who you invite to that party. They're going to become the people that are going to refer you to everybody they know for connections. You can ask them blatantly on the blog:

"Hey, I'm trying to get to some people, some angel investors. Who do you know that knows somebody that knows somebody that would sit down with me and at least give me some advice on where to find some money?"

Basically that's the crux of it. The thing is, to find people that you can do something for, as simple as the laminated little thing, that's cool. There are all sorts of people that need stuff done.

A friend of mine got involved in the speaking business big time and got on national stations with big speakers because he went to some of the largest promoters. He was a sound guy. He knew about sound and AV. He went to these people and said "Hey, man, you're paying $20,000 to have some guy come in and report on your seminars every time you do one." "Yeah, right." "Well, why don't I come do them for you for free? I like you guys." "Okay!"

When he asked later, he said, "Hey, I have a presentation. I want to become a speaker now. I'd like to speak to some of your audiences. Would you mind, at the end when everybody else is done, giving me an hour on your stage to talk to your audience?" They almost had to say yes! Once he was out on the stage, he did well and now he's moved up in the schedule. He's a national speaker and he's pretty famous. He got there by doing something totally free for somebody. Whatever it is that you do well, do it for those people. Do it to help them out. Give them something. They're going to give you back a lot more than you give them.

The Chick Filet founder guy Truett Cathe said they gave away millions and millions and millions of pounds of chicken in samples. His whole pitch was, "You can never give away as much as you'll get back." Do the John Kennedy rule, "Think not what your country can do for you, but what you can do for your country." In the same way, "Think not what your contacts can do for you, but what you can do for them," and the rest of it will just kind of take care of itself.

It will just happen by pretty much universal law. It happens whether you believe in spiritual effect or universal law effect or not. A lot of people do, it's mathematically certain to. My friend used to send out these seven or eight clippings a day and it would cost him five dollars each day but over the period of a year he had sent out a thousand congratulatory messages to people who probably didn't get congratulated by very many people. There was nowhere in town that you could go with him that ten people didn't shake his hand. I was in a small town. Nobody liked to go to lunch with him because everybody wanted to talk to him, say hi to him, shake his hand. They were all his friends and he was wildly successful in a business that most people even hate to think about.

Centers Of Influence

You need to get to know some accountants, but they are kind of hard to get to. Everybody wants to get to them because they're the most trusted people of influence around business people. You need to figure out a way to get near accountants.

Financial planners are another obvious choice. Attorneys, especially ones that specialize in investments, trusts, and things like that. Bankers. High net-worth individuals that you know. Business owners that are successful in your industry and have been successful for a long time. This is a big one that people forget: hang out with people that you know who have secured angel investors or venture capital funds in the past. They've been through the trenches so they're going to know who to refer you to.

One thing that is cool is if you have someone who has been through VC funding and he's been successful. Everybody that passed on his deal wishes they hadn't, so he could point you to those people. If he calls up and says:

> "Hey, I know you passed on our deal. We're making a billion dollars now, noogies to you, but I have this young guy in my office right now that has this badass opportunity that I think you ought to take a look at."

It's kind of a no-brainer. These are people of influence. Everybody says, "Well, that's easy enough to say, so how do I go see a bunch of accountants?" You don't. You're going to have to limit yourself in the beginning.

Buy Your Way In

Honestly, the easiest way is to buy your way in. People deal with large law firms and large accounting firms and things like that for a reason. A large accounting firm may have 1000-1500 clients. A lot of them are high net-worth individuals, business owners, and things like that. By being a client of that accounting firm it's well within your right to say, "Can you refer me to some people that might be…?" That's how I got funded for the first big deal that I ever did for the Internet. For the first time ever I used Price-Waterhouse-Coopers, a big accounting firm.

When you go to those guys, they're going to interview you. You don't just call them up and say, "I want you to do my books. Where do I send the check?" They interview you to see if they want to mess with you or not. They want to mess with great big companies, or they want to mess with small companies who have very big potential.

The thing is, accounting fees for big companies are huge. There aren't that many giant clients out there that switch, so most of these accounting firms, the major ones – Price-Waterhouse-Cooper, KMG – have a certain set of accountants or a department in their offices where they basically grow clients. If you come in as a young guy or a young girl with a business plan and you have a start up you're not going to be able to do it for no money. They're going to want some money, but you might be able to spend $5000. That is a way that might not be too expensive but can get you a lot of mileage. You can get in.

How are they going to get more fees out of you? By getting you funded, by getting you up and running, by getting you moving. They're not going to go out and actively fundraise for you but they will make introductions for you a lot of times: attorneys and financial planners.

Financial planners are really tricky. Why would a financial planner want to refer a client to you, take money out of his stock account that he's trading, and potentially you blow up and his client gets screwed over? He has a lot to lose by referring you so you have to give him a reason, and it can't be money. I think it's against the law. You can't really give him money or chairs or anything like that. He has to disclose all of this stuff. He has to just simply make an introduction of it.

Make Referrals

The good part of an angel investment deal is if it's a really good deal and an angel investor does well, he's going to be grateful to that broker forever, but that's pretty much a stretch. Most of these guys will just play it safe. Get to know them. Do a lot of favors for them. Refer clients to them. Refer people that you know, some up and coming financial broker. "Hey, I referred you two cases. I just wanted to call and let you know, here are the people I referred to you." Do that unsolicited a few times.

The guy is eventually going to start wondering. "What is this guy's deal? What does he have going on?" When you see him out at the mixer (and you're going to see him out at the mixer because stock brokers go to these things to meet people, they're good at that) he's going to talk to you,

"What do you do?"

"Let me tell you. This is what I'm doing right now."

The reason I have been successful I because I constantly think in terms of not only how he can help other people, but what those people want. That's the mindset you need for this entire deal. That is going through every bit of this no matter how far along we go. When you understand what the other side wants, that's the only way you can negotiate. If you're wrong about what they want you're dead in the water before you ever start.

Most people assume it's all about dollars. In the end it is, but not really. Not along the path. Everybody that is in their trough, any one of these people of influence that is smart, the reason they're a person of influence is because they have somehow along the way gained the trust of these high net-worth individuals and they only want to do things for these people that help them so they maintain their trust.

Without the trust all of these professions, accountant, lawyers, financial planners, they're all out of business. The only thing they have going for them is the trust of their clients. As long as you can assure them in every way possible that you're not going to violate that trust, and that what you're bringing to their clients is a good thing, and you build some obligatory base.

To get an introduction: "Do you have any clients that could consult with me and be willing to go out and let me buy them lunch to pick their brain for a little bit?" Entrepreneurs, can you guess, love to talk. We love to talk about what we do. We love to give business advice. We love to hear about new things and new plans and dissect them and think about helping people and advising them.

Compliment, Compliment, Compliment

You don't get a guy to come to lunch with you and talk about investing in your business by just going up and asking him, though. You need to complement.

> "Hey, Bob Smith over at Merrill-Lynch told me about you and I don't know if he said anything…"

> "Yeah, he did."

> "I really respect you as a business man. I respect everything you've done."

Most people don't want to compliment people because they think it sounds gratuitous or fake. Compliments work. Compliment, compliment, compliment. There is a great book on how to be charismatic. It's a super book. Look up "How to be Charismatic" on Amazon and you'll find it. You don't even need the book, actually; I can give you the book right now. Be complimentary. That's the number one criteria that most charismatic people have. They're complimentary of other people around them. Ridiculously so. The more complimentary, the better. The more emotionally complimentary, the better.

Be genuine. It's easy to find something that you appreciate about almost anybody. One of the things they suggest in the book is really funny: "Building your compliment muscle." Most people don't compliment. Most of the time people aren't confident enough in themselves to see those things in other people.

Try to form the habit of every time you're standing behind somebody in line at the grocery store, whenever you go to the coffee shop, every time you meet anybody: find something about them and compliment them:

"I like the color of your shirt. That's nice."

"Those are really nice shoes."

"I like the way you cut your hair. Where did you get it done?"

"I heard you talking to your son over there. You're a really great parent. I really admire you as a parent."

Don't do it expecting anything back. Just do it in your everyday life at every possible opportunity you can. Eventually you'll build it as a habit. It will just become part of who you are. It kind of flows over you, and you will notice yourself elevating. It's crazy. You'll just build and build and build and build and build. What you say to that person standing behind you in the grocery store, "Man, those are really cool shoes," may be the kindest thing anybody has said to that person in a week. It probably is. People are so narcissistic and self-centered in America that nobody has anything good to say to anybody else for the most part. Just that one little thing can make you really smile.

It's funny, for a society that is so connected and so many social places to be on the Internet, we are incredibly disconnected. The socialization of the Internet is successful because we have a fear of associating in person anymore. But we have this primal need to associate, which is why so many people flock to those places.

Befriend Your Banker

Bankers are people of influence. These are people that don't necessarily make a lot of money and they don't have as much to lose either, by the way. Your lower level bank people are almost as important as your upper level bank people. The bank teller: in most cases, bank tellers or branch managers of banks have a more personal intimate relationship with their clients than the president of the bank has. You may very well be able to establish a relationship with the branch manager, or teller, at a bank and get an introduction to somebody of high net-worth while you're standing in line at the bank. Don't discount that. It's pretty important.

Pass People Over

Other high-net worth individuals that you know, almost everybody knows somebody that's wealthy. At first, you don't want to ask them for a referral, "I just want to talk to them about my thing." Don't. Pass them over.

"Hey, Uncle Milty, do you have somebody, not you, but somebody that is really smart that I could talk to that could help me out with my business?"

One of two things is going to happen. Either they're going to refer you to somebody, or they're going to say, "Hey, I wait a minute. I'm smart. Let me talk to you about it." Don't ask them directly. Always be asking about the next person up in the line. Even when you meet with your angel investor, you may ask the angel investor even though you know he's your target:

"Do you have anybody that you could introduce me to that might be willing to give me some more advice, some more insight?"

"Well, hey, hold on. I might be interested in that."

Everybody wants to be the guy, but when you ask them directly they're forced to make a decision. Nobody wants to render a decision. You're making it to where they actually chase you. If you try to convince them of something it's hard. If they make the decision on their own to pursue you it gets real, real easy real fast.

They Want To Like You

Also remember the people who have already secured angel investors or venture capital financing. Those guys are going to have an affinity for you. They're going to really like you. They really are. Groups of people who have been through horrific things together typically get along well. In the fundraising process most entrepreneurs will tell you that it was probably one of the hardest parts. The business was easier to run and start and make money with than the funding process was.

Sometimes it can be kind of hard so they have an affinity.

Ask For Advice

When meeting this guy, try to always do it with a referral, and try to offer them something for their advice. "Hi, my name is Bob. I own an auto detailing company right now…" and I've seriously seen this example,

> "…and I'm wanting to start a chain of car washes and I'd love to come out and talk to you for 30 minutes to get your advice about how I should approach my business. I'll come out on Tuesday and detail your car for you from top to bottom if you'll give me 30 minutes at lunch. I'll even buy you lunch."

It's kind of hard to say no to that! You're asking their advice and opinion. Remember those words, "I need your advice and opinion." You're already immediately showing them respect. Most people don't ask people's opinions. You get plenty of opinions without asking most of the time. People like that. Ask for their advice. Ask for their opinion, and try to do it with a referral. That is the thing that is really the most important about how you should approach.

Once you get to meet them you need to ask the right questions. I don't like the idea of always asking advice, always asking a lot of questions, but don't let the meeting go to the end without a call to action. You've got them there. They're kind of buying into your idea. They're giving you some of their advice. You can read them and see if they are excited about your offer or not.

Get More Referrals

If they don't seem excited about what you're
offering, I wouldn't ask for investment at that
point. Or even a furthering of that. I would only
ask for another referral. If you can see that they're
not into what you're doing, the very best thing you
can do is try to refer up the ladder. Don't blow
your wad there.

I guess it's sort of like dating a sorority sister. If
you're not hitting it off, are you better off to try to
kiss her, or are you better off to say, "I'm a Star
Trek guy. Do you have any girls in this sorority
who are into Star Trek?" She may think it's a great
out for her, number one. She's like, "Oh, my gosh.
This guy's a nightmare. I'd hate to tell him." Just
tell them, "It doesn't look like we really have that
much in common but I was wondering, are there

any other girls in the house that you think I'm a better match for?"

One of two things is going to happen. Either she's going to go, "Whew, I'm off the hook" or "Yeah, as a matter of fact I think Sally might be great for you. Let me introduce you." And you're going to get an introduction to Sally and another shot. Or, she may go, "Hey, wait a minute. You don't like me?" That's very, very, very likely to happen.

That may very well happen, and this investor might snap back in and start to wonder whether they should pass that deal or not: "You don't want me involved?" That's a great way to lob it across.

The Right Questions

If the person is just really, "I love what you're doing. It's awesome. This is terrific." Then there are certain questions I would ask before you go in for the kill, so to speak.

Ask if people invested in their business when they got started: "Where did you secure your investment?" "Let me tell you the story." They start telling you the worst stories, the commiseration. That's where you get started and it gets their mind where they were when they started where you are right now. That way it brings you guys together. They say that the biggest way that people bond is through mutual disaster. Holocaust victims are one. They are bound together. The Marine Corp. Rape victims go to support groups together and bond. Former alcoholics go to AA. Disastrous events or things in their lives, that sound awful. New York City after 9/11: look at how the city melded

It's all an affinity group. It was hard to get where you are. It was a lot of work and a lot of effort. If they have had to go through that it's good to get them talking about that part of the business. You know what they're probably always going to do at that point? Get excited. That was the most exciting part of their business. You can bet on it.

I was sitting at a bar waiting for a table in a restaurant not too long ago, in Memphis, Tennessee. I was sitting next to an older guy and we struck up a conversation. He asked me what I did and I told him. He was like, "Oh, man. Boy, that's exciting stuff, start-up companies and all that."

I might get the wrong number, but he was employee #24 at Federal Express. Actually, he was employee number four because they hired twenty people when they started and didn't get funded and had to lay them all off. When the company got funded, he was the fourth person brought in.

We started talking about it. He was an older guy, maybe in his sixties, and fairly low energy sitting there drinking a beer at the bar, and you could just see him starting to raise up in his seat and straightening up, his eyes got bright and he started talking faster. He said, "Let me show you something." He reached into his wallet – this is an absolute crazy true story but a great story – and he pulled out a photo of him and five other guys standing in front of an airplane with their arms stretched out forward. He said, "Do you know what that is?" I said, "No." He said, "Look at it real close." I looked at it real close and these five guys all had credit cards in their hand. These were guys that were with Federal Express, he was a pilot, and they couldn't put fuel in the Fed-Ex plane that they were flying so all five of them went in together with their credit cards and fueled the plane because Federal Express didn't have the money to pay for the fuel.

Twenty or thirty years later he's carrying it around in his billfold because that was probably the most exciting time in his life. He told me after, he said, "I'd go back and do it. My goodness I wish I could do that one more time in my life." And I kind of reminded him of that, because to him I was a young entrepreneur. He knew I would appreciate that story. He knew that most people wouldn't get it. They'd think he was crazy. I totally got it, and it was remarkable to have that talk with him.

Have A Mission

When you do get your company started and running, have a cause. Have a mission. I've learned so much in business as a young entrepreneur that I thought that was a bunch of crap. "I don't need a business plan, that's a bunch of crap. I don't need a mission statement, that's a bunch of crap." Wrong. It's of paramount importance that you know exactly what the mission of your company is. The mission of your company shouldn't be to make money. The mission of your company is to make people's lives better in some way, to better the world in some way. Your reward for that will be money, no question. Probably, if you follow that mission well, it will be money beyond your wildest dreams.

Zig Ziglar has been talking about that forever. Help enough people to get what they want, and you'll get what you want. That is just the way it works. There's just no way around that law.

What if you're talking to someone and they're just super interested?

> "I love what you're doing. I just love what you're doing!"

Then you say:

"I am looking for people to get involved on a financial basis. I have a business plan I would like to drop by for you to look at."

Don't try to close them at the table and ask for the check. "I have a business plan I would like for you to look at if you have time. Take a look at it."

Then set a deadline:

> "I can drop it off for you today at three. Why don't I come by your office tomorrow at four and let's take 15 minutes and talk it over."

Don't give them the business plan unless they commit to the appointment. Stick to that. Most people say, "Let me just drop by my business plan." "Okay." They're not going to read it. If they know they have an appointment with you at four tomorrow they're going to take the time to read it because you're setting a deadline. They're going to probably take it home tonight and get prepared for their meeting tomorrow. They'll come with a list of questions. You need to definitely set that deadline. It's incredibly important.

Come in to that meeting prepared to pitch. If you have your slides, bring them in the laptop. Don't set them out on the counter as soon as you get there, but bring those slides prepared to pitch.

Other Places To Find Your Angel

There are other places you might find angel investors, which you might want to start to become involved in. There are a lot of investor forums on the Internet. Most of the time these are angel investors that are in other parts of the country. A lot of the time, you might be in a rural area and you have to deal with somebody outside your geographical area. The closer they are to you geographically, the better, typically speaking, because you're going to want their advice and their help. You can do it long distance. I like it better close.

Entrepreneurial organizations, things like the Chamber of Commerce, Rotary Clubs, they are all fabulous places to get involved in if you're going to meet other entrepreneurs, other business people.

Trade profession associations. You want to know, "How can I find somebody into what I'm doing?" Finding an association that has to do with your industry is going to give you an immense amount of knowledge. Get their newsletter. Get their magazine if they have one. Read everything in it.

Again, if you want to grow in an industry, clip out those news articles about those people in your industry. You don't have to only mail them to your town. If you're into something that's national, if you're into the packaging business get the Packaging Digest which is a trade magazine, and every time someone comes out with a new packaging design they tell you who did it. Clip that out, laminate it, and mail it to the guy that designed that package that got in the magazine. He'll think that's the coolest thing since sliced bread. If you ever need a favor, if you ever need information, if you're ever at a trade show some time you're probably going to bump into him in the house. "Oh, yeah, you're that guy that sent me the article. Thanks." That works on a very personal level in most people.

Also, if you're looking for a list of associations you can go to www.PlanningShop.com/associations and they'll have a whole list of associations in America for just about anything.

A lot of cities and states have small business development centers which offer free one-on-one training for entrepreneurs, sort of like the SCORE organization. You can go to www.ASBDC-US.org to make an appointment with somebody in your area.

Your local chamber of commerce is a great thing to join. The chamber does mixers weekly or bi-monthly. Go to every one you can possibly go to. People that are going to be there are going to be people that know other people in your community.

Do something clever. Wear something funny, a hat or shirt. Put your name tag on upside down so people have to look askew to read it. Do something memorable. Be remarkable somehow. Don't be stupid or ridiculous. You don't want to go in a clown suit. Don't be obnoxious. There is a fine line between interesting and weird, you know?

Go to trade shows, relevant conferences. One of the things that people pass on is government. If you're in anything that is at all regulatory based, go to every government event that they put on because the people who are going to be there that you're going to meet in these classes of twenty people are going to be the people who would potentially regulate you if you did something out of line. It's a great idea to meet those people face-to-face, let them know you're conscious, let them know you're doing a good job and you're going to get a lot of good information. Plus, you can get some government contacts.

Lastly, I'm going to give you one killer, killer tip. If you're doing any kind of a newsletter or anything for your blog and you just need an excuse, call up the editor of the trade magazine for the industry that you are in who is somebody that knows the industry better than anybody, knows everybody in the industry probably better than anybody but is kind of an unknown themselves. Call them up and say,

"Hi. You're the editor of Packaging Digest?"

"Yes I am."

"Hi, this is Perry and I'm putting out a packaging newsletter for my blog and I was just wondering if I could do a thirty minute phone interview with you to put on my blog?"

They're immediately flattered. They'll almost always do it and you can ask them anything you might want to know about the industry. "Who are the five most influential people?" Ask them. That would be a great question.

"You've been in this business a long time. Who do you think are the five most influential people in the packaging industry?"

"Well, I'd have to say it would be this guy, this guy, this guy, this guy, this guy."

Guess who just went to the top of your hit list? Those five people. You can ask those questions and when you post on your blog:

> "Hey! This is Perry, the unknown guy who has never been in this business and doesn't know crap about it. I just want to post to my blog my interview with the president of the National Packing Association."

All of a sudden, you just moved yourself up to that stratosphere.

Choosing The Right Investor

After you've gone through all these different places to find them and asked the right questions and you have your list of people, who do you choose?

I'll give you my criteria of what I would use if I were you. Then it's totally up to you.

Proximity. How close are they to you? If you are in the virtual world they can be anywhere. Who cares? But if you're a hands-on person like I am, and really, when you're starting a business you're pretty much hands-on, I like to have someone close by so you can have meetings and there is not such a problem going back and forth. Proximity is really important.

Someone that you feel is comfortable with the risk. That is kind of hard to explain, but I wouldn't want to do a deal where someone was giving me $1 million in angel money and he was only worth $3 million. It's too impactful to his life if I mess up. I'd rather do something where someone is investing or risking a small amount.

I've seen this problem over and over again. You have a guy that you consider wealthy, maybe he's worth $1 million and you talk him into giving you $100,000 to get into your deal. He's giving you 10% of everything he owns. Most of his $1 million is probably not liquid, or discretionary, so that may be half of all of his discretionary money in the world. He's going to be up your butt with a power tool. He's going to be fearful of loss. You don't want a guy who is fearful of loss. You want someone that is going to be positive on gain. Most people that are investing, the best angel investors are the guys that say:

"I'm going to take two percent of my total net worth and invest it in angel money and maybe I'll hit a long shot and make a bunch of money. I'll probably have a lot of fun. If I lose it, it's two percent."

It's like golf money for them almost. It really is.

Do you trust them? That's a big thing. How do you feel about the trust level? I would not want to do a deal with an angel investor that I've met one time and not spent much time with. They're probably not going to do a deal with you that way either. They're going to meet with you over and over. I want to develop a level of trust. Ask if they've done angel deals before and how they went. Ask about their VC contacts. Who else do they know to go to the next level with? That is going to be important to you.

This is a $1 million tip I'll give you here: ask them, if they're experienced, who they've funded before. "Have you done angel deals before?" "Yeah, I have. I've done three deals." "Can you give me a referral of someone that you've funded before? Do you mind?"

Most of the time they'll give you somebody. Usually they'll give you somebody they funded and it was a success. After they've done that, ask if they've ever done an angel deal that failed. "Yeah, I did two deals that failed." "Would you mind if I talked to one of those people too?" You want to find out that if things don't go perfectly, how do they react? Do they go bananas? Call up the contact:

> "Hey, I'm thinking about doing an angel venture deal with this guy and I know your deal didn't work out. How did he take it? Did he want to sue you? Did he want to kill

you? Did he want to burn your house down? Was he like 'it happens', did he try to help? Was it all your fault?"

You're going to know a lot more about that guy if you talk to somebody with whom he has been in a deal and it failed. That's where the salt of someone comes out.

You need to find out the information about their background and who they are. You are protecting yourself as much as they are trying to protect themselves from making a bad financial decision. I imagine a lot of people get caught up in not thinking that they should be able to do that since they are the one asking for money, but they absolutely should.

You need to be humble in how you ask. You don't want to be a jerk about it, but if they're a really good investor they're going to be pretty impressed that you were wise enough to ask those questions. I have a business and if someone walked up to me tomorrow and said, "Hey, I want to be your partner, I have a $1 million check," that wouldn't be good enough. I have to know a lot about you.

This is going to be a relationship you may spend a lot more time in than with your wife or your husband. This is someone you are going to be intimately involved with for a long time. If they're nuts you need to know it. It's not a decision you should take lightly, and it's not one you should only base on dollars and cents. That's a good way of selling your soul.

Angel Investor Groups

Angel investor groups are sort of like a group of lawyers that share an office. They all have their own clients. Occasionally the lawyers might work together on a case and that's the way most angel groups are set up. Some angel groups throw money into a pool, but those kind of become venture capital companies. The way an angel group works is that a bunch of investors get together for camaraderie, talking about deals, talking about entrepreneurship. This is the entrepreneurial cult. These guys are cult leaders. They're entrepreneurial cults.

They get together in the darkened walls of a smoky room and talk about business deals all day because that's what they dig. They get together and what an angel group does is when deals come in to the group, the group meets together kind of as an informal board, and they look over what deals came in this week. "What do we have, guys? Let's read them off." They go through the proposals they received this week. "That sucks. That sucks. That sucks. Well, that sounds like it might be interesting. Let's have that person come in and pitch." They contact you and ask you to come in to pitch. At that point you're going to come in and pitch to a group of these angel investors, and one, or two, or three, or ten, or all of them might say "This is terrific and we all want in." This is rare. "We all want in. This is a $1,000,000 deal and let's all throw in $100,000 each and go." That doesn't happen too often.

Usually what will happen is one, or two, or three of the angel investors out of the group may be interested and want to talk to you further. Then you can do a break-out interview or a break-out pitch or a Q & A, and the rest will pass. It's usually better to try to reschedule with the three who are interested, or ask if you can meet with those three right after and answer any questions that they have. You need to show complete transparency and be willing to allow them to ask you anything and go through a Q & A session.

There are a couple of places online that you can go to find groups of angel investors. The Angel Capital Association is really the biggest group. There are roughly 200 members in the US. Go to www.AngelCapitalAssociation.org. Also, the Angel Capital Education Foundation, ACEF, is www.AngelCapitalEducation.org. It is an organization where they educate angel investors on how to be an angel investor. It's a little bit different. You can look in places like the phone book, or online and type in "angel investors" and then your city, or the closest big city to you, and see if you can find anything from that perspective

I like groups, by the way. They're kind of fun to deal with and there seems to be a synergy among them. I've had more success before angel investor groups than I've had with individual angel investors, just because they have come together for a purpose. They're not usually running other businesses. They're usually semi-retired.

The good news about an angel investor group is that there is almost always enough money in the room to fund your deal. If you're dealing with an individual investor you never know. This guy may be driving a Lexus, and everybody may think he's just loaded, but he may have had a lousy year in the market and owe a bunch of money to the IRS. You really don't know. He may not be able to do your deal no matter how good your deal is. Don't be disappointed by that. I've pitched deals before to people that I know they wanted to do the deal so badly they could taste it, and for whatever reason they didn't. Then I found out later that at that particular time they just couldn't do the deal. They don't want to tell you. They're kind of embarrassed to tell you because you approached them with such respect. They don't want to say they can't do your deal because they're broke. That would be the person to let off the hook by asking for a referral.

Finders

I have one warning: there are some people out there called "Finders," who are financial matchmakers that claim to match you with angel investors and with people who can give you money. They want to put together a deal and charge you 10%, blah, blah, blah. The pitch is typically, "We'll put you together with a bunch of investors and we'll only take 10% of the deal if it happens."

This all sounds good and then it gets down to some point where they say they need to put together all your financial records and they need a $2500 or $5000 fee to do all of that. For the most part they are charging you a fee for putting together some paperwork, and they don't have any contacts. It's a pretty big rip-off. You need to be really careful of those organizations. If you do decide to use one make sure it's one that comes highly, highly, highly recommended with tons of references. Call those references and verify them and make sure they are for real. As a rule, I would tell you that the finder industry is riddled with fraud so you need to be really, really careful.

Selling Your Idea   9

Behind The Idea

Of course your idea is important to an angel investor. It is important, but venture capital companies don't buy ideas. They invest in business models or businesses. They don't invest into ideas. There's an old story that the only thing valuable in the world is an idea, and there's a lot of truth to that. However, without execution, it's not worth crap.

I had a lady one time who gave me one of the best compliments that I ever got in my life. She said that if you were a baker, you could have all the ingredients to make a cake: flour, sugar, milk, eggs, and all that; but the one thing you can't make a cake without is heat. You've got to have an idea; you've got to have a chef; you've got to mix up the ingredients; but then you have to execute. That's the heat: the effort. The idea is important, but without a plan to execute, it's hardly worth crap.

There is good news. I say this and people say, "Oh, yeah. Sure," it's really true, though: there is *so* much more investment capital out there than there are reasonable places to put that capital. If you're one of the few people who get it (and after reading this, you should) and you create the proper plan, put together the right package, and have an idea and a market that really works, you'll find yourself in a competitive situation where you'll have investors approaching you. The word will get out. You can have a lot of investors to choose from because there is a great deal of capital out there. People don't want to be left out.

Business Models

So yes, your idea *is* valuable, but without a compelling, executable business model, you're never going to get it funded. You're going to have to actually sit down, take your idea, and figure out how you move it into the marketplace, how you turn that into a business, and what your systems are going to be, all the way from marketing to delivery, to customer service, to retention.

Also, you can have a great idea for a brand new amazing buggy whip, and it's just not going to work out. You're not going to get funded because the buggy business kind of sucks right now, and it has for about a hundred years. Large markets with high growth potential are what angel investors and venture capital investors look at. For the most part, they are really not interested in commodity-style businesses: grocery stores or things like that.

You're not going to find a lot of VC money or a lot of angel money for that. You might want to go back to fixed conventional financing. That's really what fixed conventional financing – like SBA loans – was invented for.

I'm not saying you can't raise money if you have expertise in an area and you have a brand new innovative idea. A great example is Whole Foods here in Austin. That's a company that raised venture capital. It raised a lot of capital, and I believe it's now a publicly traded company. They're in the grocery business, so they just defied everything I said. However, they're in a completely different style of the grocery business, being in the natural, all-organic, all-health business with cafes and a bunch of other things. They found a different way to deliver on the grocery business with a whole different set of income streams and real high gross profit margins versus the traditional grocery store models that are low. Yes, you can still be in a traditional business, but it's definitely got to have an interesting twist to it.

Industry Growth

They also look for the growth of the industry that you're in. That's extremely important. That would, again, go back to Whole Foods. The growth of organic foods, organic food consumption, people taking better care of themselves, and stronger health is rapid. It's on fire, and it's an under serviced industry. Remember this. You have a product and you think that if you can sell so many dollars worth of that product a year, and you can do it for twenty years, you'd make a billion dollars. The truth that most smart people know is that whatever product you have is probably not going to be a viable product in three to five years.

Write this down in your book. This is incredibly important: the value of a company is its ability to continue to come up with new innovative products for its marketplace.

Creating A Cult

Look at a company like Apple. What if they had stopped at the Apple computer, and said, "Oh we've got this Apple computer and it's awesome"? They could have sold Apple computers to schools, and their growth would have stayed flat. Eventually, they would probably have become extinct. However, they grow into more and more products. They create markets. They continue expanding their market bubble from computers to graphic users to music to cell phones to movies and entertainment. Do you see? That bubble just continues to get bigger and bigger and bigger, but still with that same Macintosh style.

A huge part of business is, "Can you create a cult?" You need to be in a business in a growth area where there's already kind of a cult following. By cult following, I don't mean the weird people who dress in black. A great example of cult following is Harley-Davidson motorcycles. Facebook users are a cult following. Don't quote me on the numbers, but it's something like this: the average Facebook user is on Facebook for an average of about 40 minutes a day. That's versus the average website that they hit and they're off within ten seconds. eBay had that for a while until they just made everybody mad. They're still doing okay, but they just went on a mission to tick off their customers and their vendors. They have a cult following, though, and people get addicted. It's like Home Shopping Network and things like that.

Constant Development

It's a business and not a product, so you're going to have to continue to come up with new products all the time. Even with Google, as hot as it is right now, everybody wants to know what's next. What are you going to do next to make money? Companies like Microsoft have been around forever. They have a reputation of continually coming up with better and more products introduced in the marketplace and increasing their share.

You can't walk in and tell an investor:

> "I have this product and I'm going to sell this same product for the next hundred years. It's going to be awesome. We're going to make a lot of money."

Most of the time you're wrong: you're not going to sell it for that long. If you're right and it becomes a product that sells for twenty years, you're going to start drawing competition like flies to honey. Prices are going to go down, the market's going to become competitive, and your product is going to end up becoming a commodity.

It all starts with one great product, that's for sure. A great example is Starbucks coffee. Starbucks' model is to actually not be in the coffee business. Howard Behar just did a book called *It's Not About the Coffee*. The whole thing that Starbucks is about is about having a magnet – which is the coffee – that drags people into their stores one or two times a day so that they can sell them pastries, other foods, lunch, music, and movies.

Amazon has its own movie company now. They produce movies. They have their own record company now. They make these compilation albums that are multiple songs on an album produced by the Starbucks label. Just in music alone, they're one of the largest music retailers in the world now because of the amount of foot traffic that they get walking through their doors every day. They know that if they're in the coffee business, they're going to peak and then they're going to fizzle out. That's the way business works over a period of so many years. You're going to see that with Starbucks. More and more products are going to be introduced, and they can cross-market. They can say, "You bought a cup of coffee this morning. Would you like two dollars off a CD?"

The latest word is that you're going to be able to go into a Starbucks very soon with your iPod, and jack it into one of their computers. Instead of waiting to download songs off the Internet, you're basically going to be able to fill up your iPod in just a couple of minutes off a hard drive – boom! –

at any Starbucks location for so much a song. Just imagine all the different things that you can deliver if you have millions of people walking into your storefront a day. Their model is delivering feet into a space on a daily basis. If they sell them coffee, great. If they sell them pastries, if they sell them music, if they sell them a movie, if they sell them a coffee pot: it doesn't matter what they sell them, really. Their whole model is delivering foot traffic.

There are a lot of ways that you can stay in front of your market. It's not just creating new products, but also in the marketing itself, in how you get people to come in, and cross-marketing other things, as well. There are a lot of great products out there on marketing that will teach you that. I did one not too long ago with a friend of mine, Ryan Deiss, called the Trial Marketing System. It's outstanding, if you get a chance to get a hold of it. It's about a three- or four-hour recording that we did on the three main points of marketing. It's a

way to grow any business. It's pretty awesome.
I'm throwing in an unsolicited plug there.

Pitching To Your Level

You also need to be in the proper stage of
development, depending on where you're going. If
you're a brand new start-up with just an idea and a
little bit of proof and some research, you need to
be dealing with friends and family and things like
that. If you've got a little bit of proof under your
belt, you can go to an angel. If you've got quite a
bit of proof under your belt, you can go to a VC
firm. The point is that if you're going to the wrong
people, you're certainly not going to be attractive
to them. If you're trying to pitch a brand new,
bootstrap idea to a VC firm, you're probably going
to be very unattractive to them. Make sure you're
in the right stage of development for whoever
you're going to see.

There are a couple of other things, also. This is an important point. You need to express to them that you understand that the money they're going to invest in your business is to be used for growth. It's not to be used to buy you a new Ferrari or to ease up your credit card debt because you're strapped out, or to send your kids to private school, or to rent a new office because it's pretty. They want to know that you're going to take this money and somehow develop it into multiples and grow the business. That's extremely important. You also have to show that you're a capable entrepreneur and that you have a strong team behind you. This is absolutely crucial.

Most VC firms will tell you that the two biggest areas they see failure in is not product. They see a lot of innovative products they wish they could fund. However, they're either not in the proper market, they don't have a big enough market to justify the investment, or they don't have the proper team in place that they feel comfortable being able to grow the business to the level promised.

Return On Investment

ROI is everything. They don't care about anything else, really, other than ROI. That's from a venture capital standpoint and from most professional angel investors if they're real skilled angel investors. ROI rules. If they feel, truthfully, like they can get higher ROI on your company, they're probably going to fund you. It's just as simple as that. The ROI that most angel investor firms look for is somewhere between three to ten times their investment. Most VC firms are looking for five to ten times their investment, depending on the stage that they're investing in you.

If they're investing in you in a second round, they can't hope to get as high an ROI as they could have gotten in the first round, because it's not as risky a venture at that point. You've really proven your point. You may be doing a million or two million dollars a year in revenue, you've proven your business model, and you have a viable, solid business. Now you're just ready to expand it.

There's a lot less risk in that than there is in saying, "I've got this killer idea in a business model. Give me a million dollars." The people who invest in you at that level deserve a ten times reward. They deserve a really high ROI. This is a good rule of thumb: most companies are not going to be interested in your concept unless they figure that your company can gross somewhere between 25 and 50 times their original investment within five years. If they're going to invest a million dollars in you today, unless they feel like you're going to be able to cash flow $25 million to $50 million in your fifth year, they're probably not going to be very interested. You're going to have to gross $25 million to get the valuations back to let them get out of the company and make their five-to-ten-times ROI. You definitely have to have some high gross numbers, some high net numbers.

ROI is everything, really. Everything else is secondary, but everything else makes ROI believable. That's why it's so important you have to include it. You've got to have all the other ingredients. When we talk about valuations we're going to talk about a concept called "discounting." Basically, you're going to come in and say, "If you give me a million dollars, I can make you ten million dollars in five years." They're going to say, "Okay. If we're making five to ten million dollars a year in five years, this company is going to worth $50 million or however-many-dollars." They're going to set a valuation on what they think your company is worth. That's the best figure you're ever going to get. From there on, they're going to come in and look at your market size, your team, your skills, and your business plan, and they're going to begin to discount that figure. That's why you've got to have all the other pieces in place.

Everything that you don't complete well to the point where they go, "Okay. You're right." If they say, "That sounds a little overstated," or "These people on his team are kind of weak and they probably can't execute," or "His market size is not really as big as he says it is…" That is really going to affect how much money they give you.

The concept of venture capital and angel investing is fairly simple. There's a value that's set. Let's say that they determine your company is worth $2 million. At that point, you can decide what percentage of the company you want to sell them. That's just a straight-up game. You can say, "I'll sell you ten percent of the company for $200,000."

Most VCs would say, "Okay." If they've set the valuation, they're okay with that. Some VC companies like to have certain percentages; but, for the most part, they're willing to come in and fund whatever percentage of valuation that you think you want to sell.

Market Size

Market size is also important. If you're wondering whether it's better to be a big fish in a little pond or a little fish in a big pond: little fish in a huge pond is probably best, to be honest. Little fish in a huge pond that has a canal over here where these really weird fish swim, and they won't eat the normal fish food. They're wanting something different.

I think splintering off a large market is usually easier, just because you have a lot more data about the buying habits of that particular group. Let's say you're selling to gym goers and you've got a new idea for a different kind of gym, like a 24-hour fitness. You've surveyed gym participants and found out "What do you wish you had out of your gym that you don't have now?" They say, "I just wish it was open when I need to go. I get off work at 2:00 in the morning," or "I want to go at 4:00 in the morning when I first get up." You can take that data and say:

> "Okay, ladies and gentlemen, here's the deal. The gym business is a $40 billion-a-year industry. We've surveyed 1,000 and found out that the biggest thing that they'd change about their gym is the time. We feel that if we had a 24-hour-a-day gym, we could pull 20% market share out of this $40 billion market. Therefore, I think if we go nationwide, my market size is somewhere around eight billion dollars."

Now you've got a market share. Typically speaking, they're going to look at that market share and guess that the best you're probably going to be able to do is have about a 10-15% penetration. We're just throwing numbers out. These numbers are totally made up and don't mean a thing. However, if the market share is $8 billion, then they figure that you have the potential to be an $800 million to a $1 billion company once your business model has completely matured. Now the question has become how long it will take you to mature, and all that. They're ready to get out the calculator and start working, then.

However, if you come in and say, "Man, I'm going to be the king of gourmet cherry tomatoes." They'll say, "Okay. How big is the cherry tomato business?"

"Well, last year, almost three million dollars worth of cherry tomatoes were sold in

America. We think gourmet cherry tomatoes can make up 25% of the market."

They'll say, "Okay. You've got an $800,000 total market. If you grasp 15-20% of that market – on the high side – you've got a $150,000-a-year business." "I'd like a million dollars!" That's the time they show you the door.

One of the big problems is overestimating your market. It's real easy to do, because you want to show your market big. Suppose you had a rebel-flag pickup truck company and you said, "Here's my market size. My market is pickup truck owners." Not really. Your market is southern enthusiasts, probably deep-south states, maybe radical. They probably don't live close to a dealership anyway.

You've got to be honest about your market share. I'll give you a great example, back in the fitness industry. Suppose you came up with a fitness concept for people who were confined to wheelchairs. You wouldn't want to come in and say, "The fitness market is a $40-billion market and that's the market that we're shooting for." You're going to have to hone down. However, this is also true. They also know that the more niche you get the higher the chance is of you securing a big chunk of that market share. For instance, if you're the only provider out there for people who are wheelchair bound to have a fitness program, then you may penetrate 20%, 30%, or 40% in that total market size. Just be honest about the market size that you're dealing in.

If you shot too high, you can look really naïve. Probably the biggest fear – and justifiably so – is when people go before a venture capital board or before an angel investor board looking like a goober.

There are about a hundred ways to look like an absolute, total goober when you go in front of these people. There are things that are just like idiot alerts: "This guy doesn't have any idea of what he's talking about. Get out of here and come back tomorrow."

Believe it or not, you find a lot of VC firms that will like you and like your idea enough to say:

> "Dude, you're smoking crack. This is B.S., this is incomplete; but I kind of like your idea and I kind of like you. Get out of here and come back and see me in a week."

Sometimes they'll do that. A lot of times they won't. That ain't gonna happen at Sequoia Capital. You're going to go into some of these big firms and you've got literally one shot and minutes to make your pitch. You will either walk out of there having swung the bat and knocked it to the bleachers, or with your head tucked between your legs, feeling like the biggest dumbass on the planet.

Know Your Competition

Competition is something else you should absolutely bring up when you get in front of these guys. If you don't talk about your competition, you can bet they're going to. They're going to want to know a lot about it. They want to know who you view as your serious competition and who you think that you're just going to trample. They want to know the names of specific companies you compete with. They're going to want to know what size companies these are. There's an easy way to determine if your market is viable or not.

You might say, "My market size is $10 billion, and I think we're going to do $1 billion a year." They'll

say, "Okay. Who's your biggest competitor?"
"XYZ Company. They're in business twenty years." "How much money do they do?" "They do $30 million a year." "And you're going to do a billion? They've been at it twenty years." The idiot alert goes off again.

If there are large companies out there in your marketplace, they're going to definitely want to know about them. It's a good thing for you. It's not necessarily a bad thing. Then you can show the chinks in their armor, basically, and say:

> "This is where we're going to attack. This is what their customers don't like about them, based on our data. Here is our data. Our data is not talking to two guys in a parking lot.

> "We did an internal or external survey of 500 customers. We asked them thirty questions and this is what we found out.

"This is what people thought they lacked when we did a web survey on one of the popular websites that has to do with (whatever the subject matter is). This is the data we got from there.

"Combining this data together, we've come up with these assumptions and we believe them to be true."

You don't ever say, "This is absolutely, positively the fact," if it's not. They also want to know, in the future, what kind of obstacles that you think your competitors are going to run against, what you might run against, and how you may be able to grab market share from them based on those obstacles. There are a lot of companies right now that have been around a long time, that are really not poised for global growth. That's a really vulnerable point for a lot of companies. You can say:

"This company is a great company. They've been around for twenty years. They do a super job. They're doing $50 million a year. However, their problem is that 99% of their business is within the United States where the market is $1 billion. The global market is $7 billion, though. We've come up with a global dealership network that will allow us to distribute our products globally, rather than just in the United States."

You can be in a business that's not necessarily glamorous or sexy. At one time, I was in the stanchions business. Those are the things you see in the airport: the little posts that have the bands on them. They're crowd-control things. It wasn't a sexy business, but it was an incredibly profitable business.

Everybody else sold those through designers and architects, and made sales calls and bid on contracts. We sold them to end users direct by the web for a lot less than the other guys did because we didn't have to pay all those people. It was a very viable business. Business efficiencies are a big deal right now. "How efficient is your model?" is probably one of the biggest things you're going to want to touch on in your presentation. You have to show them:

> "We can do this better than the guys can, and here's why: We're more efficient. We have better technology. We have a more streamlined process that takes out these three middlemen. We have easier accessibility for the customer."

It's really, really important to spend a lot of time being saturated in the market that you're planning on going into, dissecting everything, looking at exactly how the competition's working.

Ask Your Customers

How can you do every part of the business better? How are you going to make yourself better? Don't just say, "We're going to do this." Say, "We asked the customer base and these are the things that they said we should do."

Everything else doesn't matter. How smart you are doesn't mean a hill of beans. The ultimate smartest person in your organization is your customer. The people who ask their customers what they want win. The ones who assume – so you make an ass out of you and me – usually guess wrong, even if they're super smart. It doesn't mean you're stupid.

I'm in the advertising marketing business now, and we advertise, promote, or market anywhere from eighty to a hundred products a year. I come up with a lot of those ideas (and I've been at this a long, long, long time) and 60-65% of the time I'm wrong. We market a product, we find out that it's not viable, we pull it off the market, and we lose money. However, when you're right you win.

Usually, it's a lot easier. You can just go back to your market and say:

> "What might you want to buy? What did you come in here to Wal-Mart to get today that you didn't find? What do you wish they'd do different? Would you rather they put the milk at the front of the store instead of the back? What if they took pennies and IOUs?"

Whatever. Common gripes are easy to find, usually. What's a common gripe in your industry, whatever it is? In the fitness industry, it was "The gym's not open the hours that I want to go." So, 24-hour fitness was a runaway hit. There were people who had different schedules and couldn't go to the gym. They'd buy gym membership and then they couldn't use it because the gym was never open the hours they wanted to go. It was just plugging the hole. It was somebody who was listening to the market and had their finger on the pulse.

The Perfect Team

The first part of the perfect team is the CEO or the leader, the founder. They're going to look at basically three or four criteria for you as a capable leader. Without a leader that's strong and that has a lot of ability at the front of these companies, the company doesn't have a shot, because you're the best it's got, for the most part.

One of the things that they're going to look at is your personality. How do you get along with people? Are you a jerk to deal with? Are you an egomaniac? They know that they've got to work with you, too. Would they want to be in business with you? Would they want to deal with you on a weekly basis and have conferences with you? Are you going to be a pain in the ass? Are you going to drive them crazy? Are you going to ask them a billion questions? Basically, are you likeable?

Secondly: Do people follow you? Do people respect you? Do you have leadership qualities? Are you ethical? Are you responsible? They're going to pull your credit rating to invest in you, probably, just to see. Do you make your car payment on time? Do you make your house payment on time? Have you been responsible in the past?
Next, they're going to want to see your track record. What have you done with your life so far? Maybe you're a college student. You're getting out of college and you want to do a start-up right out of college. How did you do in college?

By the way, people don't get this about college. If you go to college and you don't participate in extracurricular activities, you're missing the point. As an employer I can tell you that I look at college resumes all the time. I don't ever look at grades, GPAs, majors, or any of that. I look to see what else they participated in when they were in school. If you didn't participate in any extracurricular activities, you were just there to get by – to get your degree – so that you can have a right to passage in the business world. You're probably going to have a mentality that is just enough to get by and have an entitlement mentality, a sense of entitlement. "I've got a college degree. Now you owe me this." If when you went to college, you were in leadership, you did as much as you could to help, you were community-involved, you played sports, or you did whatever, all those things speak volumes to your character. Be sure to include those.

What they want to know is if you've worked at a job. "I worked at a job at Pizza Hut. I started off making pizzas and I became a driver. Pretty soon I was supervising the drivers and I became an assistant manager of the store. I did all that within a year." That's important. If you rise in any organization – no matter what it is – that makes a difference. When thrown into a bigger pond, you're probably going to rise there, too.

Next, they're going to look at your communication skills. How well do you communicate with them? How honest do they feel that you are? How transparent do they feel you're going to be in the future? Don't ever lie about anything to a VC or an angel. If you get caught in a little, bitty lie, it can blow your whole deal. Don't ever lie about anything. The odds of them finding out are pretty darned high. They're pretty savvy and they're going to ask you a billion questions over maybe eight or ten meetings. You'd have to remember everything you said. They're going to ask you the same questions in multiple ways. You've got a team of people sitting there listening to you. Somebody's going to say, "Hey. I thought you said before that …." You just blew your whole trust factor. Once a guy hands you a million dollars, he's going to want you to be honest about what you're doing with a million bucks. If you weren't honest about what kind of GPA you had in college, you're not going to be honest about a gambit when you've got all the money in your pocket.

They also want to know about your expertise in the field. For the entrepreneurial leader, they want to know that whatever it is that you're doing, you're really good at it. That you know the industry, you've had some experience in the industry, and you really understand how it works.

The other thing is that they're going to meet your team before they fund you. They're not just going to meet you. They're going to meet your team. You need to make sure everybody is singing out of the same songbook. Confusion leads to seizure, basically. This is true in marketing. When a buyer gets confused, they seize up and they do nothing. The same is going to be true with your investor. Suppose you tell them that this is a billion-dollar market and you think you can get 20% of it because of _____. Then your CFO comes in and says, "Oh, man, it's great news. We've got a $1.9-billion market and we think we can get 30% of it."

Even though that's a better number, they're going to say, "Hold on. Don't you guys have a plan? Don't you guys follow the same beliefs? Don't you share the same numbers and ideas?" Good or bad doesn't matter. Less or more doesn't matter. It's just that everybody should be singing off the same thing. They're basically going to want to know who's going to be leading the business day to day, and that may not be you. You may have a partner that's in management, and they're probably going to prefer that. Maybe you've got a partner that's a strong manager and you're the entrepreneurial, seat-of-the-pants guy.

Let me tell you: we all know, as angel investors, that you as an entrepreneur probably suck at running a company. We know that. You're an incredibly necessary part of the growth process, though. However, if you've got somebody else to run the day-to-day, we like that. They're going to want to know who's doing the financials. Who's keeping up with the numbers? Who's doing your R&D? Who's coming up with new products all the time? Maybe that's you. Maybe it's somebody else. Maybe you're in a business that's highly scientific and you have doctors or you have some sort of technical people to do that. They want to know that.

Who's going to handle the production of the products? Who's going to handle the marketing, technology, and sales? Who's in charge of the fundraising? Who should they deal with if it's not you? Who's going to be in charge of investor relations? They want a point person that they can tell, "We need updates on a regular basis. If we don't get them on a regular basis, who do we talk to?"

They're also probably going to want to know who's going to handle your legal matters.

Finally, I'm going to give you a big tip here: if you're going to a VC firm, don't waste your time until you have a skilled financial person on your team. You may still get funded, but here's the downer: most VC companies are made up of former entrepreneurs who are the investors, Wall Street-type investment-house guys that run the firms, along with accountants or CPAs. Usually, half of the management of a VC company is financial. They don't get entrepreneurs, really. They only talk accountant talk. It's a different vocabulary. You need to have somebody who they feel they can trust with the numbers. Entrepreneurs tend to massage the truth when it comes to their numbers. A lot of times, it's just honest enthusiasm. However, you have to have a skilled financial person on your team, and it's easier to get than you think. You can find somebody that's a former Big Three accounting firm person and maybe this is what they do now, or they went out on their own.

We had a lady in a deal not too long ago. She'd been an accountant at Price Waterhouse Cooper, then got pregnant and wanted to stay home with her child, so she took up sitting on the Board with two or three start-ups. She had great credentials. She was credible, smart, and articulate, and that was a really big help when it came time to get funding. Angel investors certainly would like it, but they don't always get it. A lot of the companies in really premature stages don't have a strong financial person in place.

It is hard to draw that kind of talent. However, there are a couple of things you can do now. There are firms online. You can go on and look for partial CFOs. You can hire a CFO, now, that may be $150,000-a-year CFO and say, "I need you three hours a week." He may be willing to work for you for $30,000 a year, for three hours a week. You're way better off to have a skilled CFO three hours a week than you are Jimmy the bookkeeper for forty hours a week. When it comes to the fundraising part of this business, Jimmy the bookkeeper is not going to help you at all. For three or four hours a week, the skilled CFO could really be worth it. They can sit in on VC meetings and funding meetings, and help you with a lot of different things.

Plus, they're probably going to come to the table with contacts. That's incredibly important, too.

Your Business Plan

I absolutely believe you should have a business plan. Business plans do not need to be lengthy. They don't need to be books. They need to be two or three typewritten pages. That's usually plenty. If you can fit it onto a page, you're a genius. That would be even better. The shorter the business plan the better, if it delivers everything clearly. The more clearly and concisely that you can deliver the information the better off you are.

The things that you're basically going to want to have in there include an executive summary. Who's going to be running the company? Who's going to be doing the different things?

You'll need a description of the company. What's your business model? What's your mission? Who do you plan to serve? What are your current products? What are you actually going to be offering in the market?

They're going to want to know general information about your industry, like the size of it and the history of it. They're going to want to know your target market: who you're actually trying to focus in on selling to. Who is your competition? What's your marketing and sales plan? How are you going to get the word out about your product? How are you going to get people involved in buying it? Who's going to run the day-to-day operations?

They're going to want to know about financial milestones. Where do you think you're going to be in a certain period of time, your projections and all that?

The Exit Strategy

Then, probably the most important thing in a business plan that most people leave out is an exit strategy. Most people think, "Well, I don't want to tell them that I want to sell it in two years. That would be wrong." Guess what? That's what they want to do! They want to know that you're on board with them. Then you just kind of move over to the other side of the table. You say:

> "Here's my idea. I've got an Internet auction. I've noticed that over the last few years, eBay has done a good job at selling these widgets, but this particular widget market is so fanatical that they'd rather have their own auction site.
>
> "We're going to build this auction site and we're going to sell widgets. We've already

started it and we've proven that we sold quite a few widgets with very little investment. We think we can get more customers and will sell more widgets.

"The cool news is that we think that we'll be a fly in the ointment in four or five years, once we get the company up to where it's worth $5- or $10- million. Probably eBay, Yahoo, or one of the other big auction companies will buy us to get rid of us. Our target is to build the $15- to $20-million value and exit with a sale or merger in five years."

They're going to say, "Wow. Okay. That's real cool. Let's figure out if that's viable and could really happen, and let's fund it."

Here's the difference. Suppose I come in to you and say, "Do you want to run up to Sonic and grab a burger?" You make a quick decision, yes or no.

Right? What if I say, "Do you want to go for a ride?" You'll ask, "Where are we going?" "I don't know yet." You need more information. It's totally open-ended. Where is the end? What's the goal? What's the reward? You're going to want more information before you make that decision.

You have to give them your exit strategy, what you think it's going to be. Maybe it's to go public. There are a number of liquidity events. One is a merger. That's one of the most common and probably the one that happens the most often. You merge or sell to another company. There's the idea of going public and becoming a publicly traded company. That's usually gigantic money. When that happens, that's a VC's homerun hit.

They don't get a lot of them, and they know that. They're sort of like those lawsuits lawyers have. A lawyer can have a lawsuit for some wrongful death case that goes on for five years, and they may get a

$1 million verdict. In between, they live off the $5,000 and $10,000 I-hurt-my-neck-in-a-car-wreck cases. Those are systematic. They come in and they go out. They earn a good profit on them and they pay the bills. Venture capital firms are going to bring in a lot of companies, but they pretty much know that company is never going to go public.

They're thinking:

> "We can make a reasonable investment in them. If they don't go public, we'll eventually sell them off to an M&A firm. Somebody else will buy them and we'll have a nice exit strategy."

Here's what they don't want to happen. Let's say you still have control of the company. They don't want to invest in you and say, "We've got a buyer that wants to buy you for ten million dollars," and you say, "Oh no. I'm living my dream. This is my baby. I grew this from the ground up. I don't want to sell it." They're probably going to have a clause in their contract that's not going to allow you to do that.

They want to know up front that you're not in love with the business. They want you to be passionate about it, but they don't necessarily want you to be in love with it. They're also going to want to know, "If we sell it in five years for ten million dollars, are you willing to go work for the other company for a couple of years for X-number salary to help them?" You need to say, "Yeah, sure. I'll do that. No problem." A lot of people won't be willing to buy your company unless they get some of the management to move over.

Talk about mergers and acquisitions, sales and outright selling of the company. That happens often. M&As are mergers and acquisitions. M&A

companies are typically investment banking companies. Here's what they do. Public companies buy smaller companies. They buy their way to growth. Almost every publicly traded company has a division that acquires other companies. That's how they go out there and grab the smaller niches. They don't want to go out and develop them. It costs those companies way too much money.

Coca-Cola doesn't want to go out and develop a chocolate milk brand. They'll just let the chocolate milk wars happen. Then somebody starts to become the emerging victor. Just when you're about to come into the money and before you really break through, some guy calls you up from Coca-Cola. He says, "Hey. I'll buy that Moo Juice from you for $20 million or $30 million." You say, "Oh yeah!" You sell it real quick and get your $20 million or $30 million. The next thing you know, Coca-Cola made Moo Juice their new billion-dollar brand because they put the Coca-Cola machine to it. That doesn't matter. The point is you didn't have that machine. Without that machine, you're probably never going to get there. So, let them have it and go do another one.

The happiest day in your life should be the day that you sell the company. When you have a liquidity event, you sell off a company. You will never make as much money in almost any business as you will the day that you sell it. Keep that in mind. It's a rule an old friend of mine told me. Exit strategy equals money signs.

By the way, when you're earning money out of your business, you have to pay income taxes. When you sell your business, you pay capital gains taxes. The taxes on the money that you make from selling the company are way, way, way less. You get to keep way more of that money, at least right now in the current tax laws. You get to keep a whole lot more of that money you made from the sale compared to the money you make operating the company. That's subject to a lot more tax.

A lot of these M&A firms will come in and buy your company, clean it up for a month or two – or six – and then go back out and sell it again to another publicly-traded company. There are a lot of M&A firms that are basically interim cleanup firms. They come in and buy companies for maybe five times profits. They can clean it up a little bit, make the books right, fill in some holes in the management team, and things like that. Then they'll go out and sell it for eight or nine times profits, and turn multi-million-dollar profits in six months.

Occasionally, you see companies that sell to their employees. The employees will group together, form a pool, and buy. Usually, though, it's private investors, mergers-and-acquisitions firms, or publicly traded companies that are coming in to pick up market share. Publicly traded companies are probably not going to look at you unless you're doing at least $10 million to $30 million a year on the low side before they're going to look at you directly. Again, though, a lot of times mergers-and-acquisitions companies will go out and buy three or four ten-million-dollar companies, merge them together, and then sell them to a publicly traded company as one. M&A companies can serve multiple purposes when you're trying to sell your company.

Paperwork

Here's a kind of checklist that you're going to want to have before you go in for a big VC meeting or before you really get down and dirty with these guys. You're probably going to want to get a professional to help you put all this together, like an accountant. If you have a financial person on staff already, that's wonderful. If you don't, get an accountant to help you put this stuff together.

You're going to want to have your forecasts. Do a one-year, a three- year, and a five-year forecast for cash, cash flow, and profits.

You're going to want a balance sheet of what your assets are now and where they came from. Current profit and loss, if you have any. A list of who your customers are: your major accounts and your major accounts receivable. Who do you owe? Where's your money coming from and where do you owe? If you have any loans or anything like that. If you started off with an SBA loan or something like that, they're going to want a list of the loans. A list of any assets that you have.

Next, you're going to need all your intellectual property information. If you own any patents, trademarks, or anything like that, they're going to want copies of all that paperwork, copies of all your intellectual property filings. Agreements with employees or third parties. Any kind of contract employment agreements that you've got, especially if it's from a key person in the organization. They want proof of your legal filings: your corporate structure; who owns shares now. If you've given shares or sold shares to investors, who has shares and how many are outstanding? They're going to want to know about how you plan to compensate your employees.

One of the big questions is: How many shares are you going to reserve or set back for employees or key employees? Especially in technology companies, the best way to attract great workers or key executives is to offer them a good salary and shares in the company. So, they're going to want to know how many shares you are set back for key employees.

Last, they're going to want to know who your advisers are. This is a great thing, by the way, to do before you go in to pitch to VC. If you can get four or five really strong people in your industry or your area to be on an advisory board for you, that's going to do two things for you. One is that it gives you the strength of contacts that they have. Usually, people are complimented or flattered by being asked to be on a board. It's going to give you contacts. It's also going to show the VC company that you're willing to take advice from outsiders; you're not this lone ranger maverick that's not going to listen to anybody. That's really important. It's a good thing to have.

Again, these are all things – the board of advisors or advisory committee – that 99% of the people that walk in their door are not going to have. If you want to shine like a diamond, get all that together before you go to your VC. Going to the VC prepared is probably the easiest thing you'll ever do in your life. If you go in unprepared, you might as well be standing there in your underwear. They're going to strip you down. If you actually have a viable idea, a viable market, and a real business plan, and you go with all your ducks in a row, it's not hard at all. They're going to love you. They're going to be complimentary of you. It's not nearly as hard as people think it is.

There is actually a checklist at our website, www.RaiseMoneyForMyBusiness.com. There's a list there called the VC Checklist which will show you everything you might need.

The Pitch

Alright, so you've made your appointment. You're making your way out and you're going to get in front of some angel investors and some VCs. What do you need to know?

This is where the rubber meets the road, isn't it? All the preparation, all the time, and everything comes down to the pitch.

I'll give you a tip that's not normally said. Have your elevator pitch ready. If you don't know what an elevator pitch is, this is a biggie. As you meet venture capitalists and people who are of influence and who know venture capitalists, know angel investors, or know other people of influence, you're going to want to prepare a pitch that you can deliver in one minute. In other words, if you were in an elevator with Donald Trump or Warren Buffet, what would you tell them about your business on the ride to the twentieth floor, which takes about a minute? That's not a lot of room for any ums or uhs.

Really, first and foremost, I would sit down with one single sheet of paper and develop my elevator pitch. That's something that you need to commit to memory. You need to be able to deliver it at the drop of a hat at a dinner party or wherever you are. You just have to know it cold.

Get all your points across: "This is what we do. This is the benefit to our customers. This is the growth in our industry. This is where we're going." That needs to be a clearly understood concept.

In addition to that, if you're pitching to a group like an angel group or a VC group, you're going to need to fill out their application form. They're probably going to have a form that asks you a lot of questions. You want to bring that with you when you come back if you don't send it in before. They may have requirements for you sending it in before you come before the group.

You're going to definitely want handouts for the people there. Those will include your executive summary and the complete business plan. The executive summary should probably be on top, actually. They should also include your financial statements, all your cash flow balance sheets, etc. Also included should be the resumes of the founders: what you've done in the past and all that.

There's also something that a lot of people don't use. Because I've been in the marketing business, I recommend the use of a lift letter. A lift letter is basically a letter that goes on the top of whatever you're selling somebody that recommends it. It's like "The president of McDonald's recommends us, the Happy Hamburger Buns Company." It's a testimonial, fundamentally. If you've got three or four of those that are really good, I'd use three or four of them. If one works well, three will work better.

You don't want testimonials or lift letters that say, "I know Joe and Joe's a real nice guy." Try to get them to write specifics. A lot of people will just say, "Just write whatever you want to say and send it over to me, and I'll sign it." That's good if you've got friends like that who will do it, especially friends of influence. These need to be letters of recommendation from other angel investors, people who have invested in you already, former employers that talk about how great you were, or people that you know in the industry.

I mentioned doing an interview with a trade magazine editor or the president of an association. If you've done that interview, this is a great time to call back and say, "We're going for our funding. Would you mind giving me a letter of recommendation?" Imagine. You come into a VC meeting and say:

> "We're starting this lawn care company and it's totally revolutionary. Here's a letter of recommendation on the top of our business

plan from the president of the National Lawn Care Association."

You want to have all that stuff together. You're going to go through a screening process, fundamentally, with all these firms: the VC firms and the angel investor firms. They get tons and tons and tons of proposals.

You fill out an application and there's going to be a pre-screening that's probably done by a junior member that goes through all these things. They have the automatic-tosses-in-the-trashcans. Basically, if all your "t"s aren't crossed and all your "i"s aren't dotted, you go in the circular file. If you get past the person who screens – which usually takes a couple of weeks – the next thing that you're going to go to is an actual Board screening. These VC firms and angel investor firms get together every so often – maybe once a week or once a month – and say, "We got 50 proposals last week. Here are the seven that Jimmy wanted us to look at." They pass them around the table and say, "We like this one or two. Call them and let's set up an appointment to let them come pitch." That's fundamentally the way that it works.

Fees

There is one more thing that I don't want you to freak out about. The first time that it happened to me, I did kind of freak out. Some of the angel investor firms and some of the VC firms now are charging a fee. They're charging a non-refundable deposit. It's basically to look at all your paperwork. Weirdly enough, I would suggest that you make one of the very first places that you present a place that charges you a fee of $150 to $250, as this means you're probably going to get all your paperwork together. You're not going to want to send that thing in incomplete. You're really not.

We send a lot of e-mails out. We used to market by e-mail a lot. When you marketed by e-mail, you hit a button, a million e-mails went out, and it didn't cost anything. Now, e-mails cost – through the better providers, if you want them to get delivered – a half a cent to a penny apiece. Sometimes when we hit a button to send out an e-mail, it costs $1,000. The quality of what we put inside our e-mails now is way better than it used to be when it was free. When it was free, it was "Throw some stuff in an envelope, send it to them, and see if we can get a deal." If you've got to attach a $250 check to the front of that envelope, you're going to pay a lot more attention to what you put inside it. So, don't be afraid of that.

Now, do be careful. I've heard that there are some angel investor firms and some venture capital firms out there that aren't really firms at all. They're just swindling money out of people. That happens. However, for the most part, if they're listed in an angel investors directory or some of the more reputable directories, they're probably pretty reputable firms. You can look up Google stories on them. Just type "Sequoia Capital funded" into Google. That way, you can see stories about companies that they've funded. If you can't find where they've funded any companies, you might be a little careful or call some people in the area to check them out and see if they're very legitimate. Those are the first things that you're going to do.

Be Prepared

Try to make friends with the secretary or the administrative assistant at the venture capital firm. That's a biggie. They're the gatekeepers, as we call them. You don't want to bug them, but you want to come to them from a point of:

"I really would appreciate it if you'd help me. I have a couple of questions. I'm coming to present on Tuesday. If you could answer a couple of questions about procedures and things before I get there, that would be awesome. Could you do that for me?"

Usually, they're friendly. Ask them:

"Can you tell me a little bit about who will be in the audience? Who am I going to be presenting to? Who's going to be there? I'd like to have a little more background information on them so that I can show them things about my business that they'd understand based on things in their business.

What's the format of the meeting? How long will I have?"

What's pretty common is that you're going to be able to pitch for 15 minutes and you're going to have 15 minutes of Q&A. That's a pretty common format.

It's a good thing, by the way, if you go in for a 30-minute format meeting and you're there for an hour and a half. Feel good about it. They've probably got interest in you. They don't book these things back to back. There's not another one coming in thirty minutes. These VC firms typically only see a few deals a month where they actually physically visit with people. If you run well over your meeting time, that's a good thing.

Ask if they have any particular requests for who they'd like to meet from your team. "Would you like me to bring my CFO with me?" I wouldn't even ask that, I just would. If you've got a CFO or financial person, bring them with you regardless. "Is there anyone else from the team that you'd like to meet?"

One thing you might want to ask them if you're doing a PowerPoint, is if they have a projector. There's nothing like going into a PowerPoint presentation with one of those little, mini, tiny, Sony laptops that they've got, plugging it in, and trying to have twelve people huddle over the top of a conference table to see it. Go rent a projector or bring a projector with you. Most of the time, though, they're going to have one. It's a nice courtesy to ask, however. At least it shows that you're prepared. You're literally ready to make your presentation at that point.

Here's what you're definitely going to want with you when you go to pitch: your laptop, obviously, if you're doing a slideshow. This is a biggie: your power cord. You'll need a projector, an extension cord, handouts, copies of your business plan, any other documents that you want to give out, and your business cards. Make sure you bring plenty. At the very first meeting, it's common to give everyone at the table one of your business cards and collect one from each of them. If you've got a product that you can bring with you, do.

If you've got your presentation done, there's a piece of software called Camtasia. It's an excellent idea. When you complete your presentation, you can load it to your computer and present it on your computer screen while you talk and record. It makes a movie of your presentation. If you can do that before you ever deliver your presentation to them, and give everyone a disc copy of the presentation with that burned onto a CD, along with all the slides individually burned onto the CD, it's a great thing to hand out. It really makes you stand out.

Depending on where you're pitching, dress appropriately. That's incredibly important. If you're pitching to people about finance, you're going to want to be in a three-piece suit. If you're in Silicon Valley and you're pitching to guys in tech, you can have an open-collared shirt and some slacks. Don't look like a bum. I see guys that come in and pitch in tee shirts. It shows your coolness if you're a programmer, but it's also sort of arrogant. There's nothing that says that a cool programmer can't wear a pair of slacks and an open-collared shirt. It shows a little conformity; not a lot. You don't have to be a butt kisser, but just try to dress appropriately.

The 12 Slides   10

This is the big deal. There's a reason I go through the 12 slides in the way that I do, to make sure that you do it exactly this way. I literally want you to present these slides in exactly the order that I ask you to present them.

You're going to have a lot of content about your business and you're going to want to get that content out. The problem is organization and delivery. So many people get their slides or the way they deliver their information out of order. They don't have a plan. These are psychological steps that you need to make with the people that you're pitching to. You need to definitely follow the slides that I'm going to tell you. It's just really important.

They're basically going to show your business concept, the needs that you meet, who your customers are, the size of your opportunity, the quality of the people on your team, and how much money they'll make if they decide to invest in you. That's the general point you're going to make. If you don't follow these 12 key slides, it's not going to be continuous for them. Something's going to be off. You've got to go through the psychological steps.

Slide 1

You're going to want to have your company name, a short description of your company, and the name of the presenter. Don't make your company four feet big on the screen. They don't really care. They're more interested in your short company description. This should all be on one slide, so you can't make the logo the whole slide. Make the logo the top left corner or whatever. Then put your mission in just a few words in the center of the slide and explain exactly what you do. This is where you make your one-minute elevator pitch. It's right here on Slide 1.

Slide 2

Key points. On this slide, you want to show the points that you want your audience to remember. "Basically, in this presentation, Mr. and Ms. Investor, I'm going to show you the competitive advantage that our company offers." People want to invest in companies that have advantages or leverage.

"Here's our key advantage; our unique selling proposition, so to speak.

Number 2: Here's the size of our market.

Number 3: This is the growth potential of our company.

Number 4: Here are the past successes of our management team."

You're going to have to keep to basically one or two lines to each of those points. You're going to have to be brief. One thing in here is that you're going to have to learn brevity. It's really important that you make the information you deliver to them incredibly dense. Highlight the very best. Learn how to write the competitive advantage to your company in one sentence. Learn how to use one word where you were using two or three before.

Slide 3

You can go into a more detailed description of your products or your services. You might show a photo or demonstration. If you've got a little video demonstration, you can incorporate that into your presentation. No more than about three minutes if you're demonstrating a product. Only do that if it's really technical. Just be sure that whatever you're talking about, don't use really technical terms. Don't use industry terms that they're not going to understand. In most industries, when you get into whatever it is that you're doing, you develop a certain vocabulary. Then if you start using that vocabulary with people who don't understand it – again – confusion and seizure. They stop. They stop listening. That's when the eyes glass over and they start staring at the curtains wondering when you're going to be done.

Slide 4

Who is your specific target customer and why will they want your product?

Slide 5

What's the market size? In your particular market that you're going to target, how big is the whole pie? For everybody that's in the pie, how much money are those people going to spend buying whatever you sell, not from you but from everyone who tries to sell it as well?

Slide 6

Talk about your competition: how the market is divided and why they're different from you and you're so much better than they are. Or, what your big competitive advantage is over them.

Slide 7

You really want to go into detail about your team. I would only hit detail about my top three or four team members and show their biggest accomplishments in life. Go to each one of them and say, "In a sentence, what do you want on your tombstone? What is the biggest thing you've ever accomplished in your life?" That's the thing you want to share with the group.

Slide 8

Show your business model. How you're going to distribute price, run your business, get your products to market. Basically, it's how you're going to market and deliver.

Slide 9

Your timeline. How long do you think it's going to take you to reach certain milestones in your business? That might not be money. That might be web users. That may be total hosted videos on YouTube, if you were YouTube when you pitched. Your milestone may not be one that's of a particular dollar amount. Actually, it's almost more interesting if it's not. Then you can kind of back in how the numbers are going to work. It would be a way of getting their attention? That way, they'll know you're not totally focused on just the dollars.

If you get enough fans on your website, the money will come. You'll figure out how to monetize. It's kind of hard to even realize how largely it'll come because it comes in waves if you're in a web business. "We hope to have 40 of our health food stores open in the first two years." What's your potential value? Basically, they want to know what your milestones are to reach your total maturity of your business model.

Slide 10

You're going to show your financials: basically, a brief web shot of your income statement, your balance sheet, and your cash flow projections. What do you think your cash flow projection is going to be? The one they're most interested in are cash flow projections. You might just say on one line, "We took in $100,000 this year. We have $275,000 in net assets on our balance sheet." You don't have to show the balance sheet. You don't have to show the income statement. "Here's a chart of our projected cash flow and growth over the next five years." That's Slide 10. They're going to be very interested in that.

Slide 11

This needs to show them how much you feel like you think your company is worth and how much money you think you're going to need to fund the growth that you want to put forward in your company. A rule of thumb is to ask for twice as much money as you really think you're going to need, if you can possibly pull it off and have the numbers still be reasonable. Stuff happens. You've got a learning curve. You've got time. You've got to train new employees. Start-ups are fun, exciting, confusing, difficult, and unorganized. A lot of times, it takes a year before everybody is playing on the same team. Don't guess that you're going to hire people on Tuesday, put them to work on Wednesday, and by Friday we're going to be doing business. It's not going to happen. Plan on living in this existence of chaos for a little while. Chaos is pretty much the rule; and they know that.

Slide 12

Talk about their investment opportunity, their potential return on investment. Again, "Here's our big exit strategy. This is what we think our exit strategy is." They're going to definitely want to know that. That's probably the biggest thing.

Making Your Pitch 11

Be professional. I would never curse in a presentation, even if it's just a silly little thing. I just wouldn't do it, because you never know who you might offend in there. I certainly wouldn't want to say anything that would be offensive to someone.

However, by the same token, you're going to want to use a little humor and have some of your personality shine through. You want them to start knowing who you are because likeability is huge. The fact that you're a likeable person is a big deal.

They want to see enthusiasm and energy. I can't get this across enough. Don't be a goofy idiot, but show them that you've got boundless energy. Basically, that's what they're buying. They're not buying your knowledge. They're already smarter than you, chances are. They're probably not buying your idea because they get a hundred more they could buy. They're buying your skill, they're buying your enthusiasm, your business model, and your energy to execute on that business model. They want to know if they have a racehorse that's going to be able to make it all the way around the track.

Make sure that your content is compelling. If it gets boring, they're going to stop listening. Allow them to interrupt when you're presenting. Encourage them to. Every time you make a point, look at the audience. You don't necessarily ask if they have a question, but definitely let them know that it's okay to ask questions. You might even tell them that at the very beginning of your presentation.

The Opening Line

There are a couple of ways to start. The safest way is just to basically say:

> "Hi. I'd like to thank you for giving me this time today to look at our company"

and give them your company name

> "and to meet our team. First, I'd like to introduce you to my key team members that are with me today"

and introduce them to your team. Then you want to start your presentation off with a bang. For instance:

> "The fitness club industry is a $40-billion industry, but currently there are 20 million

customers that are physically disabled across the country that can't use a traditional gym, and they're without a gym. This market alone would be worth approximately $8 billion. Right now, it's not being attacked."

Usually, one of the best things that grabs their attention is an unserviced market share. That's probably one of the biggest things that they're looking at and that you already know. That tells them you understand them. You understand who they are.

Red Flags

Some things are going to make investors just shut down and stop listening to you.

I'll start with the biggest one first: misrepresentation. Truth and honesty is the absolute most important point that I can get across to you. One of the big things is inconsistency and misrepresentation. You give out the handouts, you start your presentation, and they ask you a question. They're fanning through the handouts while they're watching your presentation. If they ask you a question and you give them back an answer that's not consistent with either your presentation or your business plan, they're going to call you on it in front of everybody. "How much money have you put in the business personally?" "I've put $20,000 in." "I'm looking at your business plan here and I only see $7,000 in cash ever being invested." "Oh, well, I put in another $15,000 worth of hard work." "Well, I didn't ask you that. I asked you how much money you put in." You're instantly a liar and your game is over. You're dead in the water.

Another mistake is over-projecting and saying that your market is bigger than it really is and just making up numbers that don't make a lot of sense. Also, they're going to be looking to see if your market is too small. They can identify right away that your market is not big enough for a reasonable investment. They're not interested in making $100,000 investment, and coming back and making $500,000 later. They're really not. Some angel investors might be, but that's odd. In most deals, an angel investor is going to want to invest somewhere between $100,000 and $250,000, and hopefully get back $1 million to $1.5 million. A VC company is going to want to invest $1 million to $5 million, and get back $20 million. So, there needs to be some meat on the bone. There has to be something there that they feel like you're big enough.

One thing that they're going to look at is you making a statement like you need to be paid back your money that you've invested already or that you need to take a big salary. When they're looking at things, they're going to say, "I see in here you've accounted for yourself $144,000 on your salary." "Yeah, that's right." "Where did you work last year?" "I worked here." "What did you make?" "I made $30,000 a year." "Why are you suddenly qualified to be a $144,000-a-year guy?" "Well, I'm starting this company." So what? They don't care. They'll say, "Why don't you do this? Why don't you just step aside and let us buy it? Let us put in a $150,000 manager that's got twenty years of killer experience and can do a way better job than you can."

Be sure to take a reasonable salary, but not something that's just absolutely crazy. Another biggie is that they do not want you to take the money that they invest and pay off debts. That's the last thing on earth that they want you to do. "The first thing we want to do is raise money to get out of this debt that we've got. We've got this SBA loan." That's not going to grow your business one iota. All that's going to do is take pressure off you and they could care less.

Another thing is founders trying to hold onto insane amounts of stock: "I want you to invest all the money that I need to grow my business, but I want to remain 70%, 80%, or 90% owner of the company." No, they're not going to do that. They're going to invest proportionally to the value of the company.

We touched on pie-in-the-sky valuations. That's saying, "My company is worth one billion dollars," or just nutty things. That's a great example. Here's where you can come up with that and get screwed up in your math. Let's say you're trying to do this concept for disabled people for a health club. If your valuation is based on the $40 billion health care industry, your valuation is critically flawed from minute one. They're going to say, "You just said that market can't service the disabled crowd." "Yeah." "Then that's not your market. This is your market over here, this certain percentage of that." They're absolutely right. Your whole valuation, your models, your numbers, and everything else in the balance of your presentation is just screwed.

You don't even want to show the slides at that point. If you can't articulate what your business is or what it does clearly and believably, that's a biggie.

Revenue Models

Make sure you show that there's a proven distribution channel, and that there are proven revenue models that you're going to follow. A lot of times, that revenue model doesn't have to be inside your business. One of the coolest things that you can do with a business is take a revenue model

or a business model from one industry and apply it
to another.

Federal Express started by taking the spoke-and-
wheel system from the Federal Reserve Bank.
How they move checks at night by airplanes is
how Federal Express began. It's called the spoke-
and-wheel system of package delivery. Over years,
the Federal Reserve Bank had developed a super-
efficient way of moving these paper checks all
over the country. That whole model, then, was
already developed for Federal Express. They didn't
have to do any of it. It would have cost a jillion
dollars to do it. They just took it straight from the
Federal Reserve and modeled into an overnight
package delivery company.

Continuity billing, like automatic billing of things,
started off in the health club industry where they
automatically ding your credit card every month.
Now, I go to a car wash where I pay $40 a month.

They automatically ding my credit card and I go get my car washed as much as I want. They basically have taken that monthly billing model and applied it to a car wash. That's a really neat usability.

Know Your Exit

Again, one of the other biggest ones is starting a business with no sense of closure or exit strategy. What happens? The investor is literally sitting there at the end of your presentation saying, "And what's in it for me? What do you want to do?" "I want to grow this business. We're going to run it and make a whole bunch of money." First, if you make a whole bunch of money, they're only going to get a relatively small percentage of it. They're only going to get money when you take money out in distribution. They don't like that.

They like to say, "We want to agree that in two years, you're okay with selling and exiting at a reasonable price." You may even be able to predetermine that price. You can say, "Look. Here's what I've got. I've invested this much time in this. I've invested this much money. I'd like to run it for two years and sell it for something over $15 million or I'd like to be merged into a publicly-traded company or maybe we'll hold and go public." Again, it's just keeping that end game in mind. They want to know that you have an end game. That's a real biggie.

Asking For Money

I would never do a presentation where I didn't ask for the money at the end, unless the presentation just went disastrously. If you just totally have your tail between your legs, if it blew up in Slide 2: "My market is all the chickens on earth!" you might want to tuck your tail and beg to go back home, polish your numbers, and come back in thirty days to do another presentation.

However, if you get through the presentation, you go into the Q&A, they're asking probing questions, and you feel that they have some sincere level of interest, I would definitely ask at the end of the meeting, "Does this seem like a doable deal to you?" and get their feel. You can't just say, "Can I come back on Friday and pick up a check?" That's probably not going to quite work out. Just say, "Does this seem like a doable deal to you?"

If they say, "Yes, it does. We seem like we're interested," I would say, "In what time frame do you feel like you could have a term sheet together?" You want to press in but leave it a little bit open-ended. Just say:

"We're going to pitch/we are pitching/we are currently pitched/we already pitched to other firms. We really like your firm and we'd love for you to be our first choice. Can you tell me within what time frame you could have a term sheet together?"

"Yeah. We ought to have a term sheet together by Wednesday."

"Great. We'll wait. I'll see you on Wednesday. Just give me a call."

That term sheet is the next step, by the way. Everything you're trying to get to in the pitch is to get to a term sheet, which still is not a check. There are a couple more steps.

Follow Up

Whether you get your funding or you don't get your funding, follow up with thank-you e-mails to all the members. Don't send them the same e-mail. Write each of them an individual e-mail if you know anything about them at all. I would also follow up with a hand-written thank-you note to each one of them. It shows that you took the time. You took the time to sit down. You're conscientious. You're probably a fairly caring person. It makes a big difference. Also, a lot of people don't get hand-written thank-you cards every day. When's the last time you got a hand-written thank-you note? You'd probably remember it. It makes you memorable.

There's a video by a guy named Seth Godin. He's a marketing guy and he has a whole pitch that he does. You can watch it on YouTube. He did it for www.Ted.com. It's an organization where big-brained thinkers come together and talk. He did this presentation on how to be remarkable. I didn't know until I watched that presentation that the definition of remarkable was that people will make remarks about your or your company later. If you've got something that's truly remarkable, that's what you're shooting for in these presentations.

Also, though, it's just the fact that you sent a neat card. Maybe you sent a neat card and something interesting inside the card. Maybe you sent a Mexican jumping bean inside the card: "We're just jumping at the chance to do business." That's called lumpy mail, by the way. You could send them something cool in the mail, where the guy says, "Hey! Come here, Joe, and look at this. This guy was in and pitched yesterday. He sent me a thank-you card. Look what's in it. It's a live jumping bean in it." It's a way to stand out. It shows your creativity. It shows that you're different. If you don't have the ability to market them and woo them a little bit, they're probably going to worry about your ability to market and woo your customers. You're not going to really offend them by pursuing them.

Simultaneous Pitching

One last piece of advice concerning this is, "Pitch simultaneously." In VC and angel investing, it's kind of weird but everyone wants a piece of the hot deal. What you don't want to do is pitch once a month for twelve months. What would then happen is that your deal has been shopped by eleven people and everybody passed.
A better position to be in is to gang up all of your appointments and pitch ten or twelve times in a week. That way you have deal sheets and proposals out all over the place. It's a super hectic

time but you let everybody know, "Hey, I'm going to be pitching over here today but I'll get back with you tomorrow. I need to see this capital company today."

This gets back to marketing. However, by doing it this way, you create a level of scarcity. Plus, there's some excitement there because all of that is happening in a short amount of time. There's a lot happening and you have a lot going on. A lot of people are willing to see you. You are one deal. It would show your level of seriousness too.

Before you go the first time, you absolutely need to rehearse your pitch. Remember your group of twenty people? Those are the first people that you need to pitch to.

> "Here's what I'm going to ask you to do. You need to get yourself in a mind frame, okay? I'm about to ask you for half of your

life savings to invest in this business. Imagine that. I'm going to pitch my presentation to you. Now, I want to know what questions you have to ask.

"It's serious, serious, serious stuff. You're going to be able to see me and one more deal. You have to invest in one or the other or you lose your money. So, you are really going to consider me seriously. What questions would you ask me? What questions would you ask the other guy coming to pitch you before you made a decision on where to place your money?"

They're going to come up with a whole list of questions that you probably didn't think about. However, that mastermind mentality will get you a long way. Individuals only think in basically one dimension. You're going to have to think dimensionally; you don't have a choice. So, try and get your group involved.

Common Questions   **12**

When you pitch, they are going to ask you a lot of questions and you need to be prepared to answer them.

Unanswerable Questions

You also need to be aware that a lot of times these guys are going to ask you questions that they really know that you almost can't answer.

It's a trust issue. They want to see if you're just going to make something up. If you don't have an answer for something, don't just fly by the seat of your pants and answer. Don't just pull things out of the air.

I have a great example of this, it doesn't really matter how your politics lean. Before, when Bill

Clinton was in debates, he'd put his fingers in front of him in a pyramid shape and pause for about ten seconds before he answered any question. This example is about really good posturing. The body language means that you're concentrating, thinking, putting together a good answer, and listening. You're really taking in the information that they gave you. Also, the fact that he paused for ten seconds before he answered showed that he was forming a reasonable answer and that he thought before he talked. It showed he was thoughtful.

Basically, if you can't answer the question, just be honest. Say:

> "Right now I don't have the information to be able to answer that question for you accurately. I can go back, work on that, and get an answer back to you as soon as possible."

You could also add,

> "If you want to know what I think I could do or what could happen, I can give you an estimate or a guess but, truthfully, whether or not that really would happen, I'm not sure."

An answer like that would be a lot better than pulling a number out of the air or making up a story that's not believable. To be honest, this is not these guys' first rodeo. This is what they do for a living; they've heard it all. They've been down the Pike with people – everything from total flimflam artists to geniuses to wackos to everything else. So, don't think that you're going to come in there with something that they've never seen or heard before.

Textbook Questions

There are a few "textbook" questions; you can practically expect the majority of these in a presentation. If you get out of the presentation and they haven't asked you any of these, you probably have a pretty big problem. If they didn't ask you any questions, their level of interest is relatively low, if non-existent. If you get to the end of your presentation and say, "Does anyone have any questions?" "No, we really don't." I would ask right then and there, "Did I do something wrong?" If they don't have questions you obviously did something wrong, missed the market, or, did something that they got turned off by.

One of the first questions that they're going to ask you will be:

"Why do you think that people are going to buy your product?"

However, more importantly,

"Why do you think that they're going to buy it from you? What competitive advantage do you have that's going to make the customer want to deal specifically with you and your company? Your product versus other products in your market place?"

In other words, to start with,

"Why are people going to want to buy your product out of the entire market; and, why are they going to want to buy it from you?"

That's your unique selling proposition. That's what is different about what you're doing. It's what makes you stand out, what makes you remarkable.

Second, they're going to say something like,

> "You know I like what you're doing but I
> really don't believe that your market is as
> big as you say it is. How did you arrive at
> your market statistics?"

You need to be ready to be challenged. They're not going to just take what you say at face value. It's like the math teacher, 16 x 34 = X. She says, "Show me your work." How I worked out the math problem was what my math teacher always wanted to see. She did this so that she knew that I didn't just look over the shoulder of the kid that was sitting next to me.

They're also going to ask you,

> "You think the market is this big and you're
> going to get this percentage of market share.
> How come? Why? Why do you think you're

going to get that particular percentage of market share?"

People sit down all the time and say,

> "This is a $1-billion market. If we just got a ten percent market share, we'd do $100 million."

> "Well, how are you going to go about getting a ten percent market share? Are you going to grow the market?"

There are basically two ways to do it. You're either going to grow the market itself and take the growth or you're going to come in and erode the market away from another competitor. However, smart money knows that eroding the money away from another competitor is much more difficult to do.

eBay grew the auction market. They're an online auction but fundamentally, they're still an auction company. The auction market was an already existing market but they totally grew a new leg. It turned out to be a giant leg on the auction market. Since they were the first market movers in that area, they were able to capture a huge percentage of the growth of the industry.

Most people that are funding usually choose that versus, "I'm going to go out and steal business away from this guy."

Do You Know Your Market?

They're also looking for how well you know your business. They want to know how well you really know your market. There's a really great show that comes on in Canada called, "The Dragon's Den." It is the most awesome show, but they don't do it here in the US. I wish they did. It's a show that comes on weekly. Seven or eight people go in and pitch their idea to a group of angel investors. The investors are all famous Canadian entrepreneurs that they pitch their idea to. The people know that they're going to be on television in front of a national audience and ten super sophisticated people. They come in and the investors ask them a basic question about their industry and the people don't know. They don't know.

People get all consumed with, "Oh, I'm going to start this business and sell this widget." However, they end up not even knowing the basics of their market. They don't know the age demographics. They fall in love with their idea so much that they don't research it out well enough. They don't know the age demographics, the sex of the buyer, the economic level of the buyer.

I'll throw in a little tip here: most of the venture capital people and angel investors that I've dealt with in the past really want to see that you're market-centric. The *if-you-build-it-they-will-come* idea doesn't really work. Everyone knows that. You have to have a market first.

Look and see the hottest things being funded in venture capital. For instance, during the "dot com" boom, a chimpanzee could have walked in with a domain name and received money. It was because there was this giant tidal wave rolling. They knew that a substandard player could jump into this arena and do well.

However, once that market is mature, it isn't going to happen. You might say, "I have a great business idea: I'm going to go in and start a search engine website. If I could just take ten percent of Google's market, I'll make a billion dollars." The thing is that Google isn't going to give up ten percent voluntarily. They're not going to say, "Do you know what? That guy is working pretty hard. I think I'll give him ten percent market share." They are not going to do that.

Bigger than that, the smart investor knows that if there's a ten percent market share out there to gain then you, being a brand new inexperienced newbie, and Google, being a monster powerhouse with a roomful of a thousand PhDs: if you're an odds player – who is most likely to gain that additional ten percent? Not you.

So, you have to create a brand new space. That's the best thing that you can do – create a brand new space. Let's take Mrs. Fields' cookies as an example of a great idea. This was many years ago but she was the first gourmet cookie chain. Keebler and Nabisco had a lock on the cookie business. They had Oreos, Chips Ahoy, et cetera. That was the cookie business. They weren't going to give up any more of the market share. Mrs. Fields said, "People will buy a three dollar cookie." Everyone thought that she was nuts until she went out to the mall and proved her point. She still has a nice market share but for a long time, she was the only fish in her pond. That's my point. She may have expanded the cookie market 10% and took 60% of that share that she grew. She was the trailblazer.

However, competition came along pretty soon after that. A smart guy told me one time, "One of the greatest places to be in positioning your business is to be the first 'second' on a hot product." Some great examples in the online world of that are, "Where is AltaVista today?" They were the hottest search engine going for a while. They were on fire; they're nowhere now. There are a lot of companies that came out and trail blazed an industry; then just went away because there were other people that were positioned. The smart observer sits back and sees everything that they're doing right. They say, "Well, that's a great idea but where are they having problems? Oh, they did this, this, and this wrong. We'll just go and do that but omit those problems." The first "second" has a real advantage, especially if they have strong management. Usually these trail blazing companies that come out got lucky most of the time. I'm not saying 100% of the time but most of the time they just got lucky. I'm from the South. The old joke is, "Every now and then the Old Blind South finds an acorn." A lot of these people just stumbled across something that was fantastic.

They may not have even known what they had. When the eBay guy started selling Pez containers, he had no idea that he was going to build a multi-billion dollar industry. By the way, he was pretty smart by turning the company immediately over to a management team. He backed out and took a chairman's seat. He knew that he couldn't run a multi-national corporation. He recognized his skills and brought the right people in.

Are You Really The Best?

They're going to ask you, "What do you think you do the very best as a company, manager, entrepreneur; what do you think your product does the very best?"

They may ask you, "If you have the greatest idea in the world, who else is doing this?" Believe it or not, if your answer is, "Well, no one else is doing what I'm doing" you better have a pretty quick explanation as to "why." That statement sets off a red flag. It goes back to what we talked about before. "I don't have any competitors." Well, everyone does have competitors, or there's no market. The market creates a vacuum. It just does.

Entrepreneurs fill that vacuum and we're really good at it.

Now, with the global market closing in, there are millions and millions and millions upon millions of entrepreneurs. In the way of market, there is very little out there where someone isn't trying to find a plug. So, when you say that nobody really is competitive against you and you have the total advantage, well, you just need to be really careful about what you say.

Why Should I Invest?

Another basic question is, "Why should I invest in your business?" Why they ask that question is to see your level of naivety. Are you going to say, "If you invest in my business you could make a lot of money back: I can probably pay you back ten or 15% a year on your investment. I'll be a lot better than a bank." If that's your answer, that's a big signal to them to get out the front door.

As I said before, they're looking for five to ten times their investment in about an 18 to 24 month period. These guys are not bank lenders; they're not looking for interest rates. They're looking for equity that returns high ROI.

Why Did You Choose Us?

They may ask you, "Why did you come to us? Why do you think we'd be a good partner for you?" They are looking to just really see if you did your homework. Early on, you want to show them that you're looking for a partner that has more to offer than just cash, which, by the way, you are. If you're not, you shouldn't even start down this road. People always talk bad about venture capital firms and angel investors. They've heard the term,

"Vulture Capitalist" before. However, with venture capital companies, you get an advantage that you don't get almost anywhere else. You go give up a lot of equity but you also now have a skilled partner, an experienced entrepreneur.

They have endless resources and connections and they have an absolute vested interest in your success. They're going to use all of those resources because they don't want to see you fail. They're going to use every resource to help you that they possibly can. This is the opposite of knowing someone who has a lot of resources but has no real vested interest in you.

So, they're going to ask you that. Hopefully you can tell them:

> "I've researched you and have seen other projects that you've done. I've also seen how you've helped these other companies. I

think that we're in a similar market place. You seem to have the right connections. I've researched your board members and their prior experience and I think that they'd bring a lot to the table for me."

They don't want to come and run your company so don't give them the impression that you want them to come and run your business. That's not what they want at all. From the beginning, they're looking for somebody that they can tell has really thought through this process.

What About Your Competition?

They're also going to ask, "You have a great whiz-bang. What's going to keep your competition from knocking you off?" This is becoming a bigger and bigger area: basically, barrier to entry. You need to show that the competitor is going to have a significant barrier to entry.

This is where "team" comes in big time and you need to show that you have the proper team to always be the best, not only for today. You may be coming out and getting start up capital and there are three other start-ups doing what you're doing. Let's say that you have three YouTubes coming to the table and all of them are doing video hosting and the same thing. Then the big decision is going to be made. Who is going to have the most progressive team that will keep this thing constantly updated, being managed well, and getting better? At that point a lot rides on the team.

What they really want to see here are things like strategic alliances. For instance, I know a client who does streaming online training. Their big barrier to entry is that they have a contract with the American Bar Association or with a bunch of the

State Bar Associations. So, they have a long-term contract with these associations. They don't have particularly proprietary technology but it would be very difficult for someone to go around to all of their locked-in relationships.

It may be technology that is proprietary; it may be patents that you have. It might be strategic alliances or relationships that you have. What they really want to see is that you have an unfair advantage on the playing field because they don't know you. If you think about it, it makes all the sense in the world. They know that you're a fledgling start-up guy. The odds of you going out and "slaying the dragon," who has been out there for a long time and knows the market place and customers; who already has a base and cash flow; and who has been doing the same thing that you're proposing to do, is really difficult. They know that. So, they really want to see that you have some big advantage.

It also can be business model. However, for the most part, business models are easily duplicated. For example:

> "We have this cool way of selling grapefruits that no one has thought of before. We're going to put them in individual plastic packages so people can take the grapefruits to work with them."

How long do you think it's going to be before all of the grapefruit sellers do the same thing?

An example of a big strategic advantage is the Dutch Boy Paint Company. Dutch Boy was just about out of business, they were an inch from it. However, they came up with the paint can that had a handle on it and a pour spout. Everyone else had the big metal paint can. They came out with the plastic paint container with the spout on it. You can pour it out like a pitcher of milk or kool-aid. That solved the problem of having the paint drip down the sides of the cans. It was a deal changer. The company went through the roof and is back on the top of the paint business again. It was because they changed that one functional problem. Plus they had a design patent on that container and all the tooling already done. They already had retail distribution so no one else can do that for 17 years. So, if you believed in that concept, and that they were going to sell more paint than anyone else because of it, would you want to invest in that company? Remember, they have a 17-year lock on it. Of course, a lot of companies did.

What's Your Marketing Strategy?

They're going to want to hear your marketing strategy, how really doable your thing is. "What's your marketing strategy?" You need to have a nice little one minute pitch that explains exactly how you're going to get the message of what you have out – how you're going to refine your market and get the message to that market.

We talked about Triad Marketing not too long ago, but: message, market, media. That's the deal.

1. What's the message you're going to deliver?

2. Who is your market?

3. What media are you going to reach them by?

"We're going to do these oversized postcards, we're going to direct mail them, and we're going to send them to paint contracting companies to show them our new paint can."

It's a good idea to have something that you've already tested.

> "Here's our marketing piece, our preliminary test show with a mailing of thousand pieces. We have a 6.4% response rate. Here is the list of the respondents. Here is how we followed up in a follow-up sequence. Here's who bought and who didn't and here's why. We went back and surveyed them and found out this is 'why' they did or didn't buy."

That's the kind of data that they're going to look at and say:

> "How many did you mail? A thousand, right? Okay, you mailed one thousand of these and it cost you $500 to mail them. You sold $5,000 worth of paint at a 50% profit. So, you made $2,500 on $500, right? How

many more places like this are there that you can mail?"

Hopefully a lot. If you have a mailing list of two or three million that you can acquire that's a similar mailing list and you can convince them that it is similar. Then you're a locked deal. It's a no-brainer for them. If you've proven a model on a small scale that's not easily duplicate-able, but is very scale-able, then you almost have a locked deal.

Why You?

Another good question is,

> "I assume you want to be the CEO of the company, right?

> "Well, what have you done in the past that would qualify you as the CEO of a large

corporation? Do you think that this company is going to get to $50 million? You graduated from college two months ago and have been working at the Whataburger.

"So, what do you think qualifies you to be the CEO of a $50 million company?"

I think what they really want to see there is some entrepreneurial spirit:

"You know what? This is my idea. I've tested it and proven that I can make it work on a small scale. I believe that I can do it on a large scale, too."

You need to let them know that you realize, though, that you're going to need qualified help. A lot of these guys are going to want to know that if the company gets to a point where it's way out of your range that you won't be a bear to fight to let them bring in a real CEO and run the company. Honestly, as much as you're out there saying, "They're going to take my company." You should know that most people that I know who have made a lot of money working with VCs have gone in, formed the company, and run it for a while. They then let it get to the point where it's kind of out of their hands, and let the VC company help them. They go in together and agree on a CEO, bring in a very experienced management person, and they then take a backseat.

It is just like the gentleman did with eBay. He took a backseat. Then, you go and relax. Now all of the pressure that you had is one the CEO's back: it's his problem to perform. To be honest, they'll probably do a better job than you; you just have to know it. I like to sing. I love to sing country music. However, I know that George Strait is a better singer than I am. I'm never going to be that good. So, if I had a certified absolute couldn't miss country hit song, I'd much rather give my song to George Strait and let him go make me a couple of million dollars than to try and sing it myself. No one would listen to me sing. That's where that is at.

Negative Questions

There are a lot more but those are some of the biggest ones. They're going to ask you some negative things, too. "What weaknesses do you see in your management team?" That would be another good chance to be honest and transparent.

What you want to do is to defend. Your natural instinct is going to be,

> "Oh, we don't have any weaknesses; we're great and terrific. No matter what happens,

we can cover everything. We have it going on."

They just know that's not true. They know it.

If you're coming in with a brand new idea, one of the big questions is always, "Is it going to sell?"

> "Oh, yes. We think we're going to sell. Every time we touch a hundred customers, we're going to sell ten. We're going to make a billion dollars."

> "Well, how many have you sold so far?"

> "Well, we haven't had the money to go out and do the big marketing tests yet to try it out."

> "I thought if you sent a hundred pieces of mail, touched a hundred advertisers; or

shook a hundred people's hands that you'd sell ten."

"Well, yes; yes we would."

"Why haven't you gone out and met a hundred people yet?"

Then what it looks like is that you're just basically there to get money to coast on. Think about it – if someone came to you and said:

> "Hey, if I go knock on fifty doors this afternoon, I know that I can sell ten people something for $1,000. So, here's what I want to do: I want you to loan me $10,000 so that I can go and get twenty people to knock on doors."

Would you do that? Or would you say,

"Heck, let's go get in the car, knock on some doors, and see if what you're saying works or not."

Then it's pretty easy to come back to you,

"Hey, I went and knocked on fifty doors this afternoon. Here's $10,000. Now I'd like to borrow $100,000 to have ten more people to knock on doors with me."

Do you see how much different the equation is? It's so much easier.

Okay, getting down to the end now. They're going to ask you two questions that are just ugly. "Who do you think would be a potential buyer for your company?" I'm not talking about a buyer for your product:

"In three or four years, once you have matured this thing, you realize that as an angel investor or venture capital one, our money has made an exit strategy, right?

"Who do you think might be in the market to buy a company like yours if and when you're successful?"

You're thinking exit strategy on the frontend. They're going to ask a question like that.

What If It Doesn't Work?

Then, one of the hardest questions to answer is, "What happens if it doesn't work?" They want to make sure that you have a disaster plan.

"When you go to broad testing, what if you find out that your small testing worked but your big testing doesn't? You have a $1 million from us in equity, you burnt through $700,000 of it. You can't figure it out. What's Plan B? What are you going to do? What are you going to do if it doesn't work out, if it's not peaches and cream?"

This is basically damage control. A great answer would be:

"Number one, we're not going to go out and spend $700,000 of the $1,000,000. We're going to continue testing.

"I know that you guys want return right away, but to be honest with you, I don't want to risk a lot of your money that you give me for the first 90 to 120 days. I want to test more before I take significant financial risks so that if I run into a major problem, I've taken the minimal amount of risk and amount of loss possible. Even if I only do this much business, you will easily recoup the small percentage I've spent. There will no minimum net negative loss."

This way they know that you're not just looking to go out there and blow their money hoping that it works. It's basically called, "risk avoidance." They want to know that you have a risk avoidance plan. A lot of people who get venture capital money say, "Okay, I have this money. I'm ready to go and roll the dice. I'll put it all on red. If I win, I have twice as much; if I lose, it wasn't mine to start with."

That's exactly what they want to make sure you're not going to do, something stupid like that.

Basically, that's the majority of the questions that I would say are going to be asked. Those are the ones that you really need to be prepared for. However, you need to know that they're going to ask you very pointed questions and most of them are going to be about the holes in your presentation. One thing that you really want to do – and, most people will never mind it – is say:

> "When I give my presentation, do you mind if I turn on my voice recorder because I want to remember the questions that you ask? I want to make sure that I answer all of them and get back to everyone."

They know that you can't take notes or write while you're doing the presentation. This is just like the Post Game Show for football games. They go back and watch the tapes of the game. That's how they learn how to play better games for the next week.

You will actually remember to follow-up on specific questions. That's something that goes a long way. Also, chances are, you're not going to pitch it once and get all of the money that you want. I hope you do, but chances are you're not. I always recommend that people pitch to the lower people on their list first. If you get a lot of offers to come pitch, you should pitch to some of your smaller funds, less likely funds first. This is because it's going to give you some experience before you go and talk to the fund that you really, really want.

Valuations   13

Valuation means, "What is your company worth?" When an angel investor or venture capital company comes in to invest in you, they're going to invest in you based on what you're worth. They're basically going to ask you, "What would you be willing to sell part of your company for?"

If your company is an idea and not much more, then it's going to have a minimal value. If it's a proven idea, it's going to have more value. If it's a proven and tested idea, it's going to have yet more value.

If you've actually entered the market, then that's different. Stages of investment are different but basically, what a company is going to do is to have you do some earnings estimates. You're going to estimate what you think your gross sales are going to be and what your net profit is going to be. They're going to look two or three years out and say, "Okay, if in two or three years you're making $2,000,000 a year." They are then going to look at what they figure they can sell that company for in two years.

For instance, let's say that you have a business plan that shows you're going to be making $2 million a year. If they feel like they're going to sell out to a Mergers and Acquisitions Company, then they are probably going to sell it somewhere around five times earnings. That means your company evaluation might be $10 million. If they think that the IPL market is really hot for what you're doing, they may sell for twenty times earnings. They may feel like your company is worth $40 million.

Then they have to also take into consideration how much share they have of the business. If, for instance, they're investing $1 million and think that in two years you're going to sell for $10 million and they get 50% share for $1 million, then they're going to basically get back $5 million in two years. That is within their perimeter of what they want to see.

However, what gets taken into consideration is discounting. Your estimates are going to get discounted based on a number of factors. They're not just going to take your numbers at face value by saying, "Obviously, if he says that he's going to make $2 million a year, there's no question at all that he's going to do that."

They're going to go back and look at historical trends and things they've seen in the past. They'll look at what causes companies to miss milestones. That's when they start discounting.

They have another strategy to dilute your shares down called "dilution." That's in case you don't reach your milestones and it helps to insure that they get their ROI. However, it doesn't help to insure that you get yours.

Valuation Factors

Valuation factors are the things that determine what your company is worth in the eyes of the investor. Number one is the size of the market. That is always your number one valuation consideration.

What is the size of the potential market that you can penetrate? Again, that doesn't mean that it's the size of the cookie market; it's the size of the gourmet cookie market. They are looking at the revenue and dollars.

Probably what Mrs. Fields did was to come in and open a cookie store in a mall and said:

> "Okay, we're surprised in this market place. There are $1-million's worth of cookies sold a week but in the mall, we have one little store and we're selling $10,000 worth of cookies a week. We have a 1% market share in one little store. So, we think that if we open a bunch of stores nationwide, we could have one percent of all the cookie market and it's a $10 billion market."

So, that's how they justify their market. That market didn't exist yet but they'd proven that they could carve it out in a very small geographical area. The thing is if they can repeat that.

They're going to look at the experience and skills of the team – how they've performed in the past, what they've done well or done poorly. A lot of it is that they're going to look at the team's accomplishments. So, when you're putting a team together, the fact that they have skills is important. However, the fact that they've accomplished something in the past is probably more important. You personally want to know what their track record is to be able to display that

They are going to look at how doable your business concept is. How realistic is what you're trying to do? If it's logical, that helps. If it's semi-proven, or proven, that helps a whole lot more. However, just because it makes sense on paper... well, I can sit down with a piece of paper and make you believe practically anything makes money. With enough imagination, you can make anything work on paper.

When you look at some of the sports teams out there, they look great on paper but then they get destroyed by the right team or by the right coach. So, it's very much like sports management really.

They are going to look at who might be willing to buy you and how big is the market for somebody who wouldn't want to buy you?

Are you in an industry that's unsavory to where public companies wouldn't be interested in acquiring you?

Are you in an industry that's on a decline where the companies that are out there – the big players in the market – aren't really actively acquiring right now? That's a big deal.

They're going to look at how strong the IPO market is. Could you potentially be an IPO candidate? For a VC firm, that's a home run hit. They don't figure that they're going to get that out of most of the deals that they do. However, if they occasionally can get an IPO out of a deal that they funded, it makes up for a whole lot of screw-ups. My buddy, Ryan, calls that a "slack adjuster." They potentially can invest $1 million in you. If you go IPO, and they do everything right, they maybe could make $100 million back. Then they could afford to screw-up 99 more deals and still be okay. They're going to look at your IPO likelihood. If your IPO likelihood is high, it definitely helps. After they fund you, how much money do they think you're going to need in additional funding? Typically speaking, what happens is that as additional funding comes into the deal, the founder's and the primary funder's shares get diluted based on how much more money you bring in.

For example, say I'm going to invest in you. So, you own the company right now. I'm going to buy half of your company for one million dollars. Now you own half and I own half. I'm an angel investor and you're the founder. We now each own half. Things have gone super great and it's now a year down the road. However, we realize that we're going to have to have $5 million more to make this thing work.

That might be something they've discounted in the beginning for. It depends on how you're structured. Sometimes they're going to have some things called "Non-delusion clauses." It is something to be very careful for. They may have it under contract that your shares get diluted and theirs don't and, by the way, that's very common.

So anyway, we need to raise $5 million more. We have to sell some shares. I look at you and say, "That's fine if you want to sell some of your shares. We're keeping ours." That would be on the founder then. So then you would end up with 25%, the new round of financing ends up with 25%, and I end up with half. That's very possible.

However, they're going to look at that. Usually there is some dilution required on their part in those situations. Also, as more cash comes in, usually the valuation of the stock really goes up so they don't mind that so much.

They want to know, "Do you have a lot of customers on your list right now? Do you have customer relationships? Do you have vender relationships as strategic partnerships like we talked about before?" "Do you have the National Bar Association in your pocket?" That's a big deal.

For example:

> "I want to open some hair salons."

> "We're not really interested."

> "I have a nationwide contract with Wal-Mart to put one in front of every store."

"Okay, we're interested."

"We have a locked contract; they won't let anyone else come in but us."

Do you see the difference in the deal? That's a major, major, major difference.

They're going to want to know the stage of the company development-wise. The earlier the stage of the company, the less risk they're going to be willing to take. It's all about, "What have you proven?" It's all back to the proof.

The stages of the company are based on, "What have you proven?" If you're bootstrapping, you've proven it works on paper. If you're in first round, you've proved that it will work in a focus group. For the first main round of financing with VC, you've proven it'll work in a local market and/or niche market. Then, by the time you get to the second round, you're trying to roll out to the national or global market in a big way. You need a lot of funds to do that.

They're going to look at if you have patents, trademarks, processes that are proprietary. Do you have pieces of software technology that can't be easily duplicated? Kind of like, "What real estate do you already have?" so to speak.

If you're in the hotel business, do you have some prime land already? Perhaps that is your advantage.

"I want to build hotels."

"Well, we're not really interested in hotels."

"Yes, but I have a prime piece of property on the Las Vegas Strip and another in downtown New York City on Fifth Avenue."

"Well, that's a whole different ball game."

They're going to also ask you things like how you price-wise and profit-wise compare with your competition.

Lastly, they're going to ask, "Have you made any money yet? What have you sold? What activity level are you at?"

When you're into things like medical technology, a lot of that may come down to, "How far are you down the regulatory route at all?" There are a lot of companies in the medical field that raise money based on how close they are to an FDA approval: they haven't made a cent yet. It's really weird in that field, it's, "How well have you managed your losses? Have you got to Stage Three of Clinical Trials and have only lost $100 million? You're doing a great job." It's such a different paradigm. They know that if you get through that, after you get approval, you may make billions. So, the up-side is extremely high so they're willing to accept some frontend downside. If you're managing the downside well, they're probably going to be okay with that.

In the online business a lot of it is about customer acquisition. Google's valuation was insane before they ever put the first ad up. They had a multi-hundred-million plus dollar evaluation before they ever took in a cent in revenue because they had millions of eyeballs, millions of daily users. It wasn't a matter of whether they would make money when they started monetizing that; it was a matter of how much money they'd make.

Now, I don't know if this is what happened – because no one ever knows what happens at Google – but, probably what they did was say, "Okay, we're going to run ads today on a million searches and see what happens." That was probably over with in 30 minutes. They said, "Okay, we ran ads on a million random searches today. We made $50,000." That was really all that they had to do. They have 300 million a day and growing like a rocket.

Do you think they had a hard time raising money? Who wants to be a part of this? Get a number and stand in line. There's no question that they were interviewing VCs. They had an auction process to sell their stock at IPO. People bid insane money to buy their stock. That really proves a point. They only had to prove what they could do on a very small scale but they proved their market size. Then they proved their ability to monetize. That's really it. Everything else from there was upside.

Pre- and Post-Money Valuation

There's a definite difference between post-money valuation and pre-money valuation, and post-value money valuation is what really matters. Your company is going to be worth a different amount of money after you're funded. For instance, let's say that you've determined your company is worth $1 million based on some of the equations that we've just laid out. If a company comes in and decides to give you a half a million dollars, they roughly should own 33% of the company.

That doesn't make sense right away, does it? You would think that they would own half. The reason that they'd own roughly 33% is because post-money – once they've given you $500,000 to put in the company – at that point, it's equity inside the company; it's working capital. So, your company is now worth $1.5 million dollars. If they want to invest $500,000 they're fundamentally buying one-third of the company. It works a little bit differently. That's the post-money valuation.

The Stages Of Business

What stage your business is in makes a big difference to how the valuation is set. I'm going to give you a round number on each of these stages. This is certainly not saying that this is what your deal is worth, but these are averages that you see along multiple deals.

The first stage is the Bootstrapping Stage. That's where you're actually putting in your business plan, travelling to see your competitors, researching, and really just spending most of your time putting together a package. You're really understanding your market, getting yourself super-duper educated. That amount of money is going to be minimal. It's probably going to be what you can raise at your party, so to speak. However, for a couple of thousand bucks you should be able to really put together a good package, research your market very well, and get your ducks in a row. That money is going to come out of your pocket and family and friends. The good news is that you typically don't have to give up any percentage of ownership or if any, it's very minimal. That's really nice.

The next thing that you're probably going to do is go out and seek some seed money. This is the Seed Money Stage. This can still be rich relatives and friends. Or, maybe you could go back to your group of twenty people and say, "I've determined that the average on this next round is going to be around $50,000 to $150,000." You may go back and say,

"Hey, I decided to go out and begin seeking funding. I'm going to need $100,000 to get through the first round of everything. This will basically get my first focus group proven. I want to do some focus groups and develop prototype products; I want to get my products out to the market in a limited way to see what the response is. I'm going to gather some data and really get some 'rubber meets the road' real deal information."

The smartest people that you'll ever deal with are your consumers. They're going to tell you what they want. For the sake of argument it's $100,000. You're probably going to go to angel investors for that. You probably won't have to give up a lot of percentage for your business either. It'll be somewhere around 20 to 25% of your business and that's pretty reasonable. That's not too painful but that is if you've proven something in your

Bootstrapping Stage. This is especially true if you have some proprietary technology or something like that. There are actually quite a lot of people out there that will share a deal like that. Two or three guys will throw in $30,000 a piece and roll the dice on you. It's not any money to them, although it is a lot of money to you.

By the way, in the Seed Money Stage, you're probably going to have to hire some people. You're going to really develop your marketing plan out and begin marketing your product. That's the second stage.

The third stage is a Series A Round. Typically speaking, it's where you're going to go to an angel fund or you may even go to a VC fund at this point. You have your complete marketing plan done, working, proven with limited statistics, and you've made some sales at this point. You've generated some cash. You have your corporation set up and you're a company. You're operating. Basically you're in business but you need funds to grow.

So, for example, you've opened one restaurant. You've proven that barbequed eel is the new big trend in restaurants. In this one market place you took a ten percent share of all restaurants with your new eel restaurant. You're whipping out your eel burgers. You've proven that you can take a percentage in a market or two and if you can prove it in two or three markets, that's better yet. If you have one each in Austin, L.A., and New York and you can prove that all three are pulling roughly the same market share, then you're able to go back and say:

> "This is what I have – three restaurants. Each one of them cost $20,000 to open. I've made back my $20,000 in three months and

I'm steadily holding a ten percent market share."

Then you have something to go show.

> "In this round of financing, I'd like to bring in equity investors for another $350,000. I want to open twenty more units. That's what I'm going to do with the money. It's total expansion money."

Remember that they're going to want to give you money for expanding only. You need to burn that into your brain. You're in debt. You borrowed a bunch of money. "I'm willing to pay off my credit cards. Can you invest some money?" "Screw you. No way." They only want to invest money that's going to multiply. If you're going to pay your credit cards off, there are no multiples that come from that, other than the multiples of the hours you get to sleep at night. It doesn't have anything to do with their money.

So, basically, in that round you can probably still hold on to control, in most cases. If you have a good solid plan it will see you raising $300,000 to $400,000. You may give up 30-48%. At that point I try not to give away control. You're going to get around to that, don't worry.

Lastly, is your second round – your Round Two financing. Or, some people call this "Series B Round." This is basically where you've proven – now you have twenty locations of eel restaurants and they're all still running steady. However, you're not really a manager; you're an entrepreneur. Some things are slipping through the cracks. Everything is going good but you go back and say:

"Here's the deal. I've proven this concept. My Eels on Wheels food carts are kicking butt all across America. However, I don't really know how to run a great big multi-national company.

"So, here's what I'd like to do. I'd like to raise three million dollars, hire a good executive staff, go out and open a hundred more restaurants, and just really blow it up. Then, in three years I'd like to sell out to Wolfgang Pug because he's going to realize the growth potential in eel is insane.

"He's going to realize pretty soon that eel is the big deal, so let's go ahead and get a big team and a bunch of restaurants open. Let's start being a pain in the neck, cutting into the market share of the other guys to the point where Red Lobster or T.G.I. Friday's or some big restaurant chain is going to come in and acquire us."

So, we want to borrow $3 million to do that. At that point you are almost surely going to give up control. That's just part of it. Actually coming in to let them know, "I plan to give up control" is not a bad thing.

However, there are some things to be considered when you give up control that kind of suck. Typically speaking, the people that you're getting funding from have a lot more money than you do. They can stand not to draw money out of the company. They're going to try to leave as much money in the company to make it as attractive as they can for a big-ticket sale in the end. The downer for you is that if they're in control of the company and decide not to take out money, then there won't be any disbursements. So you don't get to take out any money.

The best thing that you can do is to negotiate a really good employment contract for yourself at the beginning of each of these deals. You can say:

> "Hey look. I'll still sit as the Chairman of the Board. I don't care how soon we sell the company. I'd like for it to sell for the maximum amount, just like you. However, I need to get $100,000 or $200,000 a year salary while we wait."

That way it makes them feel good that you're not going to be banging on the door daily saying, "Man, I really need cash. I really need cash." The last thing that they want to do is strip the company of cash. They're going to try to take that cash to fuel growth. They know that the faster that they can grow, the more they can get out there in the market place, the bigger target is placed on their head.

Mergers & Acquisition Companies and Publicly Traded Companies

Once your company gets to the point – well, there are different levels. Companies over about $10 million get attractive to Mergers and Acquisitions Companies. These are companies that basically put together groups of companies and, most of the time, sell them to publicly traded companies.

A public traded company typically won't buy a $10 million company. They'll buy a $100 million company, which may be a grouping of ten $10 million companies. For them, the cost to acquire is very expensive because the publicly traded companies have to pay for incredible due diligence. They have to integrate all of the accounting and management; it's a pain in the neck. A $100 million company probably costs them somewhere between $3-$5 million – it's just a bite. It probably doesn't cost a whole lot less than that for them to buy a $10 million company.

The Mergers and Acquisitions Companies is a really interesting business to be in. The guy that heads their acquisitions department knows exactly what it's going to take to make life easy on the publicly traded company. So, they're going to buy your company – pull it into their fold – and put it into the right accounting software. They're going to get the right management and financial people onboard. They're going to get all the reporting and SEC documents all ready. They're going to have everything all packaged up in a nice big pretty box with a bow on top. This is so that when that publicly traded company says, "What do you have?" They are looking. There's a lot more money even at that level. I'll say it again. There's a lot more money especially at that level. There's a whole lot more money out there than there are deals.

I'm going to try to explain a principle here that's a bit hard to get across to a lot of people but imagine this: Most publicly traded companies are trading at somewhere between twenty and forty times earnings. Some are as many as a hundred times earnings. These are high tech companies.

On the low side, let's just say that a publicly traded company's share price is worth twenty times earnings. If they acquire a company at ten times its earnings, the instant they acquire it, it's worth twice as much. It's a way for them to grow. In other words, if their stock collectively is worth $100 million and you have a company that is earning $10 million a year. If they have your company it would be worth $200 million to them. So, all of a sudden, instead of their stock being worth $10 a share, it's worth $30 a share.

It instantly increases their value by a multiple of somewhere between 20 and 50, depending on what they were trading at. So they have a person who sits in an office all day and looks for companies that they can acquire for less than 20 times earnings; that fit their market plan; that have a synergy with them. They're usually going to buy a company that maybe they're a distributor of whole foods, for example. We have one here in Austin. They probably target buying vitamin companies, organic farms, et cetera. This is because they can not only buy them and get a big flip on the multiple and then they can distribute their products through their distribution channel. There's a synergy there that works. Blockbuster Video bought Paramount because Blockbuster could distribute Paramount films.

Those are the best deals although that's not always the deals that get done. There are some companies out there that are just literally big cash vacuums. They acquire practically anything that's pretty.

So, we'll use the example from before. Your company is making two million dollars a year. An M & A Company may come in and pay you five times earnings, even though your books are kind of weird and your team is weak. They know that by this time you, as an entrepreneur, are probably freaking out. They know you're freaking out because you're in over your head. You would really just like to cash out. So, when they hold out $10 million in cash, and say, "Oh, $10 million..." while they shake it in front of your face. It's more money than you've ever possibly seen. You're going to snatch it up. They just bought you for five times value for $10 million.

They can probably go in. They bring in these teams of troubleshooters. There are short-term CEOs and CFOs. They're going to sweep into your company and fix everything that's wrong in six months. They'll package it, dress it out, and make it all perfect, and in six months time, they're going to go to a publicly traded company and say, "I have this gym over here that I can let go for only twelve times earnings." They instantly flip it. You made $10 million to start with but they just made $10 million in six months for knowing how to package it and where to go to sell.

It's not a question of whether they can sell it or not; it's a certainty. These M & A Companies are being bombarded by publicly traded companies. Their acquisitions teams are saying, "What do you have? What do you have? I have to feed the Pike." This is because there is constant pressure for incredible growth out of publicly traded companies right now. In most companies only about half of growth comes from sales and activity. The other half comes from acquisition. So when you understand that whole concept of how the cycle works.

I know that this is kind of premature for most people who are reading right now but it's a good idea to understand how the whole system works. If you really see the end picture, you see what other people are looking to gain. You need to realize, too, that when you're buying stock on the Stock Market, you're paying absolute retail. So, M & A is in the wholesale business.

There is wholesale and sub- wholesale. The publicly traded company that has an Acquisitions Department is in the wholesale business. He's buying watermelons for five dollars and selling them to you for ten. There's a guy in between that's buying them from the grower for two dollars each – that's the founder. He's then selling them to the publicly traded company for five dollars so everybody in between is stepping on somewhere and making money.

A lot of times in these deals you can maintain positions and seats, you can move up. If you're an integral part to the operation you may want to do that. Sometimes people will sell based on gaining experience or based on getting themselves in the door of a publicly traded company. If you're needed enough, they like you enough and you're doing a good job, you may get a long-term employment contract and a seat on the Board. It would be a good idea to have a plan for seeing yourself as part of the picture, if you want to be.

A lot of times they're going to really want to know that. I had a company one time that I had put my heart and soul into. I could hardly sell it but I'd moved onto other things. A lot of people looked at it and said, "If you're not going to stay, we're not interested in buying because you are the company."

While you want to be a dynamic figure in leading your company, you definitely want to start very soon in getting people trained to know what they're doing. You want to prove to them. Last year I took a month off and went to Hawaii. I actually had a sales increase while I was gone. Everything ran better when I got out of the way.

That's a big deal for an M & A Company; or, for a publicly traded company because they know then that it's the system that's working and not the person. They'd much rather buy a working system. Does McDonald's make the best hamburger in the world? No. However, they have the best system in the world at selling hamburgers. The system is worth billions. You can make a better hamburger and sit next to them all day but they'll beat your brains out because they have a better system.

Aim High

There is a lot of fluff that goes into valuation. I would always give people the advice to aim on the high side. Don't be ridiculous but aim on the high side.

I was with the great entrepreneur, Guy Kawasaki. He's responsible for tons and tons of start-up sales. Not too long ago I was at a conference with him. There was a speaker there. They speaker was a VC for one of the largest VC firms in the country. He said,

> "Do you know what? When you come in and do these two-, three-, and five-year projections, and you're all sitting at home at night trying to figure out what you're going to put on the piece of paper. You say, 'This

is just bull shit. I have to come up with this; this is bull shit.'

"Do you know what? We know its bull shit. We just want to know the magnitude of your bull shit."

How much do you really believe is over the top possible? Don't make it insane where it can't be but in the best-case scenario of everything going perfectly well, how much money are you going to make? You need to base your valuation on that.

They're looking for people who aim very high. When Kennedy said, "We're going to go to the moon" everyone thought he was from the moon. "Nobody can go to the moon. Come on." Then, in less than ten years, we were on the moon. They realize that if people set goals that seem unreachable but have passion and believe in them, they can usually accomplish them.

However, it takes part of your soul with it a lot of times. They don't want to give that up but they'd love to fund you and let you work 90 hours a week to accomplish those things. Let you get the arrows in your back. If they can let you take the arrows and they get some "cha-ching" in their pocket in the end, everybody's happy. They'll let you facilitate the dream.

Term Sheets 14

One of the cool things about working with a VC is that you learn how real business runs. They are going to issue something called a term sheet. As you go through different stages of funding and even at the point you get to a buy-out, you may actually get a term sheet.

A lot of people in merchant acquisitions and things like that use term sheets. A term sheet fundamentally spells out all the aspects of the deal so there is nothing left to chance. They have to disclose everything to you and you have to disclose everything to them. Due diligence means they get to investigate and make sure what you have disclosed to them is true. You can also perform due diligence on the company you are accepting investment from and you want to do that.

I am going to give you a little heads up on what you might watch out for and what parts of the term sheet are negotiable and what parts usually aren't. Really, most of the term sheet is considered negotiable. The term sheet is put together by the issuer, the person who is actually the founder of the company. It is the person who is issuing stock to the investor. That is where it starts.

Debt and Equity

If you are borrowing the money, you are the issuer. Then they will talk about the capitalization of the company and its worth, both pre-money and post-money. That will be part of it. You are going to talk about the type of arrangement it is, whether it is debt or equity. In most cases, what we are going to talk about with VCs and investors is equity. They are going to buy a percentage of shares for a certain amount.

Occasionally, you can structure a deal where you will accept some investment and some debt. In other words, they might want a 25% ownership share and give you a certain dollar amount also be willing to facilitate a loan at a certain percent so you can have working capital outside of their investment.

There is something you need to be aware of and beware of it. Some angel investors and some VC companies will want to invest in your company, to purchase shares simply for signing on a line of credit or signing on a debt instrument.

Basically, that's like me saying:

> "You need $100,000. I'll tell you what I'll do. I'll run down to my bank, we'll sign together on it, my bank will give me $100,000, and I'll give it to you. You go do

the business and I get half the company and the company can pay the debt back."

That's pretty expensive money. You will get the interest and the debt service and you are going to give up half of your company all at the same time. Typically, when they do that there will also be something in the contract that says if you default on the debt, they can convert it to equity and probably take all of the assets of the company. Those are usually pretty lousy deals. You don't see a lot of reputable VCs that try to float deals like that. Those are usually pretty shady companies that do that sort of thing.

Negotiations

There are some things that are really not up to negotiation. These are things like information rights. You will talk about how transparent you are going to be with them. The answer is that you will be very transparent.

When you get down into the contract and begin to negotiate, there are some big things that are negotiated first. Usually it starts with valuation. How much is the company actually worth? You have to have that amount as a starting point for everything. I hope everybody understands that you don't just say an arbitrary figure. You can't say, "I want this much money and I'll give you this many shares." That is typically not the way it works. Everybody has to agree on a valuation. They have to say, "Today we think your business is worth this." You may think it is worth a different amount and the truth is probably somewhere in between.

You are going to take your estimates at face value and say, "I think it's worth $10 million." They will take your estimates and apply discounting to it. They may say:

"Your numbers show you are worth $10 million, but you haven't really completely proven your business model on a large scale, so we need to discount it by 10%.

"You really don't have a strong financial person on your team, so we are going to discount another 10%. You don't have good books and records, you don't have any real track record, you're only a couple of months old. We're going to discount it more.

"You don't really have any protection of a competitor coming into your marketplace, so you may not have a very long future, so we're going to discount it some more. Now we think it is worth this amount."

Then you negotiate. At the end, you are going to say, perhaps, the company is worth $1 million. At that point, you determine how much you want to sell and they determine how much they want to buy. You may only want to sell 20% for $200,000. They may want to buy 50% for $500,000. You have to decide how much of a partner you want at that point.

To be honest with you, for VCs anyway, the deal has to be pretty good sized for them to go to all the trouble. They're going to spend a lot of man hours checking you out, checking out the opportunity, helping you, and working with you. They know they are going to have a heavy investment of time. Venture capital companies really don't want to do $50,000, $60,000, or $100,000 deal, for the most part. Venture capital companies do $500,000 to $2 million deals. Angel investors, a lot of times, will do $100,000 to $250,000 deals, but usually only when they think their angel investment is going to go in, in six or eight months you are going to go to venture capital, and their angel money is going to be worth a whole lot more. Their shares are going to be worth a lot more once you are fully capitalized by a venture capital company.

You are going to negotiate the equity division, how much you want to sell. You're going to negotiate the employee pool. You will want to set aside some stock to give to key employees. This is the standard now among start-up companies, particularly tech companies. Let's say there are a thousand shares. You want to set aside 10% of the shares right at the beginning as an employee pool. They may want you to set aside less; you may want to set aside more. You negotiate on that.

Then you split what is left over. You may not be splitting 100%. You may be splitting 90%. You reserve the other part because later in the transaction you may need to give a CEO a salary plus 3% of the stock in order to attract a really good CEO or a really good CFO and have smaller stock options for less important employees.

Anti-Dilution Provisions

One of the big things to watch out for is anti-dilution provisions. These are things like warrants. This gets really tricky, so I am going to try to slow down and explain this one well. Basically, some contracts will be anti-dilution clauses. Let's say they invest and they get half and we get half, right? They are probably going to attempt to have an anti-dilution clause which says that in the future, if you decide to sell more of the company to raise more money, you take it out of your shares, not their shares. You really want a deal where you take it out of both shares. That is really mostly fair. If they feel like they are at risk with their capital, they may not be in agreement to that. These people for the most part are not unscrupulous. They are going to disclose it: it's there. However, you need to understand what it means.

Using A Lawyer

By all means, don't ever, ever, ever agree to a term sheet without consulting with a very good lawyer. That is really super important. It can't be Jimmy, the guy who handled your car accident when you were eighteen. You want a mergers and acquisitions lawyer, somebody who has a focus on business law and specializes in it. It will be the best money you'll ever spend.

A lot of times these lawyers will do deals that are back end loaded, if they think the deal is going to come together. They'll say, "I'll tell you what, let me charge you a $1000. If your deal all comes together, you pay me $10,000." A lot of times they'll do that. They might not do it as clearly as that. They might do it based on you using them for future services. Hopefully, they are going to grow a client out of you. You might be able to say:

"Hey, look. I have this deal right now. I'm trying to get VC funding. I have a lot of appointments and there's a lot going on. If I get this through, I'm going to need a lawyer to help me with my affairs for years to come.

"Right now I'm a poor kid without a lot of money. Hopefully, I'm going to have a lot of money. If you want to take a shot and help me out with this thing, I'll give you my word that I'll use you for as long as I can as my legal counsel."

Any decent attorney, for the most part, is probably going to be open to that. Most people actually do like entrepreneurs, folks who are trying to do something. Usually, they will be pretty amenable.

Employment Contracts

The next thing you need to look out for and make sure you take care of yourself is employment contracts. Usually, VCs are pretty reasonable about giving you an employment contract. You need to know that if you've been in your business for a while and every time you wanted a new motorcycle you just took $10,000 out of the bank and bought one, it is not going to be like that from now on. That money in the bank is equity. If you take $10,000, you have to give them $10,000. That's number one.

Number two, they're probably not going to want to take a dispersion. They don't really like taking money out of companies: they would rather you multiply that money and parlay it back in. The way the VCs see it, if you're multiplying money four or five times a year, every dollar you take out costs four or five. The reason this all works is because businesses grow the most dynamically in their first two years. A business may grow by 2,000% or 3,000% in the first two years. If it starts out with $10,000 and grows 2,000%, it is $2 million. If you spend half of that the first month, it's a million. You could spend $10,000 and it cost you a million down the road. That is what they are looking for.

With employment contracts, ask for a very reasonable salary. Don't ask for something stupid, for way more than what you need. Ask for what you need. They will want you to live comfortably. They don't want you to be starving to death. They want you to be able to stay focused on the business. You need to say:

> "This is what I have. These are my expenses. It costs me about $6,000 a month to live, so that's about $72,000 a year. I'd

like to have some wiggle room, in case I need something or an emergency comes up.

"I'm going to be traveling a lot. I want to look nice and dress well to present myself and the company well. I don't want to look poor to my employees. I want to drive a nice car. How about $100,000 a year? Does that sound okay?"

Most of the time something like that will be okay as long as you can present a reasonable argument for it. If you say, "I want to make $200,000 a year because I think I should," and you don't really tell them what you need, you're taking money off the top before they get theirs. They're not getting a paycheck. What you're saying at that point is:

"Hey, here's the deal. I'd like you to give me all the money to start this business. I'd like to take out my salary plus I'd like $100,000 of return a year out of the business while you get nothing."

You are more worried about your personal gain than you are considering the company. That is why you want to negotiate a good employment contract. I'd say a three-year term is a pretty good term. Also remember that if something came up in the negotiation stage, like saying you wanted $200k, they can yank the deal any time they feel like it. These term sheets are not binding. They're just saying what they propose.

The Vesting Schedule

This is a term used in venture capital and angel investing all the time. Vesting means you are going to own 50% of the stock and they are going to own 50% of the stock. Usually vesting only applies to you. This is not always the case, but usually it is. It means they don't want to give you the money and you go out tomorrow and sell your stock in the company, cash out, and they don't have anybody to run the company. They potentially lose. A whole lot of what they are investing in is you as a founder. It is your team.

A good example of a vesting schedule would be three or four years. Typically, they'll say, "You have stock that is now worth a million dollars. It is a $2 million deal and you have half of it. We're going to vest you at 25% right now." In other words, if you really wanted to, you could sell $250,000 worth of your stock. If you could find somebody to buy it and you really wanted to, you could do that and it would be okay with them. They will usually give you another two points or so of vesting every month until you are 100% vested.

Let's just say that takes 36 months. At the end of that many months, you could potentially sell all your stock, if you wanted to. You may not have fulfilled your employment contract. Employment contracts go both ways, remember that. They are agreeing to employ you for a certain amount of time and you're agreeing to perform, not to only be employed and sit there like a lump. If you don't perform to the best of your ability, you are in violation of the contract.

You usually want your vesting schedule and your employment contract to end at about the same time, if you can. That way, if you're ready to move on and do something else, you can sell some of your stock out, get out of your employment contract, and make a clean break. Your vesting schedule is important. Again, the standard is about three or four years with 25% up front.

Liquidation Preference

This gets really hairy. A lot of times, they will ask to get back all their money first in a liquidation event. In other words, it is first in, first out money. If you liquidate, for whatever reason, for less than what they invested, they can get it all. There are accelerated liquidation clauses, too. In the initial contract they will say, "We're going back to the situation where I am buying half of your company and paying a million dollars." I might have a two-times escalation clause which says that if we have to liquidate, I get back two times my investment before you get anything. Let's say I invest $1 million. You fail quickly, we get in trouble, and we have to liquidate. The company is worth $1.2 million and even though I only invested $1 million, I get the whole $1.2 million.

They will justify that in the negotiations by saying, "Look, your deal has significant risk of failure." The way you try to get around that is to prove to them as much as you possibly can that there is a low risk of failure. Prove there is a good exit strategy. If things don't go your way, what is Plan B? If you have a good Plan B, they may not stick to that as tenaciously.

Selling Clauses

There is potential for there to be clauses in the contract. Let's say, for instance, the company is worth $2 million. They may have a clause in there that any time in the first year, if they can find a buyer for $6 million, you have to sell. If they find a buyer in the second year for $10 million, you have to sell. These clauses are in most contracts, believe it or not. You will not be able to say, "I don't really want to sell. I like my work." They don't care. If they see a spot where they can exit with a five or ten times return quickly, they will do it.

The windows of opportunity you have to do that are sometimes pretty limited. To be honest with you, they don't really need the money as much as you do. If they think it is the optimum time to sell, it is probably the optimum time to sell. It's what they do. You are better off to say, "Great. Awesome. You found me a buyer at $10 million? Let's sell this thing. Bring me my $5 million check and let's all go home happy." The next day you go do something else.

Once you learn how this game is played, you can do it over and over and over again. This is really important. Once you've done one of these, your first one, you want it to end in a quick exit strategy with a positive result. The second time will be that much easier. As they say in the south, "It is a can of corn." Just walk into the next VC deal. When your last VC deal was funded at $1 million and eleven months later was bought out at $10 million, it will take you minutes to get funded. You'll have competition to fund it. That is the whole deal. If you're listening to this, you are probably going for your first deal. With your first deal, you need to let them know you are on board to get out. You want to drive it up, dump it, and move on down the highway. The quicker the exit strategy for the biggest pot possible, that's what you're in for.

Control

This next thing hangs up a lot of people. I'm talking about control. Most founders freak out about not being in control and not having controlling interest. Michael Gruber calls it the technician, where it is their baby and they don't want to give up control.

They don't want to give up 51%. They'll give up 50% or 49% all day. The 50% deals get done, but they are hard deals, believe it or not. The unfortunate part about a 50% deal is that there is no decision-maker. Things can really go undone for a long time and that can be really harmful to a company. They don't really like 50% deals. They like 25% deals and 35% deals pretty well if they trust you because they are not very exposed. They can help you as much as possible without putting a whole lot of money out.

I would say that a big portion of the time they are looking for a controlling interest if they go over $1 million. If you have some super, red hot technology, some super lock-down patented something or other, the hottest thing that is really smoking on fire, everything is very negotiable. If they don't take control, they will at least want some board seats and they will probably want to place some of their own people. The most common is to place their own financial person: they will want to hand pick the CFO. It will be someone they know and trust and someone who will not pull the wool over their eyes. Again, they are protecting their interest and ultimately the success of the company. They will probably do a buttoned-up, tight contract on that person where you can hardly fire them. Any time you go in to talk dollars and cents with them, you had better know exactly what you need and why.

I've been a situation like that. I was still the majority stockholder of a company, but I had an adversarial relationship with the CFO, someone a VC firm had placed in the company. Let me tell you, it was difficult, it was challenging. The exit of the deal was not pleasant. Everybody made money in the end, but it wasn't a lot of money. It was kind of ugly. I would almost rather they had control. They would have felt more comfortable because fundamentally they had control anyway. They put the financial person in place and you can't control the financial person. They are holding the purse strings, so who is really in control?

The big problem in that particular company is that the president of the company and the CFO were making different decisions one from another and it really hurt the company. What was really awful about the situation, though, is that the CFO was making the real financial decisions, but the CEO had all the liability for the decisions because he was the president.

It can really put you in a weird position. You need to think about all these things when you are negotiating control. Here is my biggest advice and easiest advice: don't freak out about giving up control. Get a good employment contract and if you give up control, it doesn't really matter. Make sure you get all the funding you are going to get before you give up control. Try to give up control on the second round of funding. Don't give it up on the first round, if you can prevent that.

Milestones

The last thing and the one that gets most people is milestones. All VC deals, all angel investor deals, are done based on milestones. Do you remember how they ask you for those projections? There is a double-edged sword. You want to make them big because you want to make a lot of money, right? You're going to say:

> "Man! They're going to give me all that money! They're going to give me $5 million and I thought I was going to get $2 million. This is awesome!"

You're going to be so excited. When you get down to the final deal sheet in your negotiations, they are going to whip those projections back out. They're going to say, "Remember what you said here? Your one year projections are to make a million dollars, right?" "Yes, that's it, absolutely." "Do you still believe that?" What are you going to say? You're in a box, right? If you start negotiating down, they will start negotiating your value down. You say, "Yeah, absolutely. I'm going to do it." "Okay, you're sure of it, right?" "Yeah." "Well, then you won't mind, then, if you don't hit those milestones if we take more shares."

If you have really overshot, you can get yourself in trouble. They will have milestones. You can say that they're being rotten and all that, but they really are not. They're just protecting their money. They're putting up risk capital and it's high risk capital. They are saying:

"You're saying you will perform and that's great. If you do, we'll live up to our end of the deal. We'll give you all this money and we'll do it for this amount of shares. If you don't perform, we will want more shares. With every one of those milestones you miss, you will lose more and more control and have fewer and fewer shares."

They will have greater interest and greater control relatively soon if you miss a couple of milestones. They will have majority interest, most of the seats, and the control. They can boot you out and you can bet they will. Your milestones will also be in your employment contract. Not only can they take more shares from you, they can fire you and put you out of your own company. It has happened to a lot of people.

Do you know what? Sometimes it is cool. If you're a knuckle head, it is almost better for them to can you and kick you out. You keep 20% or 30% of your stock, get a job somewhere or do something else, and maybe they will turn your company around. They are pros. They will bring in a bunch of hired guns and they may turn the company around and sell it for $10 million in a year or so and you get a $2 or $3 million check.

So, when you are going through the process, you want to make sure your projections and your valuation are somewhat in line. That is the balance that should keep your projections realistic, yet ambitious. That is the best possible way I could explain it. You want realistic, yet ambitious, projections.

Due Diligence 15

I want to quickly hit this ugly thing we call due diligence. This is the ugliest part of using a venture capitalist. This is the part people don't really like. There are ways to simplify it and I'm going to try to simplify this for you, so you can make it easier on yourself.

Checking You Out

There is a difference between angel investors and venture capitalists. Angel investors are using their own money and venture capitalists are using other people's money. They have particular rules they have to follow. They don't have a choice but to follow these rules. There is a whole checklist of due diligence and they are going to check you out. They will check to make sure what you said is true. Don't be offended by it because they are investing other people's hard-earned money into your business venture based on their good word. They really have to check you out; they really don't have a lot of choice. Don't be surprised by this.

They are going to call on a variety of people like attorneys, accountants, and market researchers. They might call on industry experts. It depends on how much money they are investing. They may hire a consultant from your industry. They may say:

> "We don't really know the bio-man industry this well to find out if this product is the whiz-bang product this guy says it is. Why don't you look at what they have and tell us what you think?"

They may have a business valuation expert from that industry come in. He may say, "Yeah, it's awesome stuff. As a matter of fact, it is so awesome that three other companies brought it out last year." They might not know and you might not know if you haven't done all your market research.

There are things you will want to have ready for them to make this process easy and quick. Have an updated copy of your business plan; have all of your marketing materials, your press releases; have your market research assessment and the studies you've done. You would have all your corporate records, your articles of incorporation, minutes, stock holder certificates. Have a record of who owns stock and who doesn't and all your business contacts and suppliers. They will probably want to talk to them. They will definitely want to talk to your strategic partners; people you have long-term deals with that lock you in, like the Bar Association.

They may want to call the Bar Association and say,
"This guy says he has a great deal with you and a
good relationship. What do you think about him?"
If the Bar Association says, "What are you talking
about? I never heard of this guy," then you have a
problem. You want to put in correspondence that
has gone back and forth between you and them and
so forth. They will want to look at any loans you
have and any financial obligations.

They will want to make sure you don't have
obligations you haven't disclosed. That is a biggy.
If you have debt, you better show it. If you owe
people, if you have leased things, if you have
obligations you need to let them know. If they find
out after the fact, it will be a deal breaker. They
going to wonder, "What else is this guy hiding
from us?"

Now, because we live in such a sue-happy,
regulatory environment, another big thing is

looking at your potential liability. Is anybody trying to sue you? Has anybody tried to sue you? Could you potentially be violating somebody else's patent? Could you be using proprietary software you are not supposed to be using? What could happen that could make this deal blow up in their face?

They will want a list of all your property, all your assets, and everything that the business owns. They will want to know all your intellectual property. Specifically, what is the specific technology you own, the specific patented items you own, or pending patent items? What is your intellectual property? What is the mass you have, the knowledge you have?

They will want employment contracts on your employees and resumes on all your employees with references. They will want to see your benefit

plan because they want to know what your
employees are going to cost.

Burn Rate

There is something in this business called a burn
rate. In all these things they are looking for your
burn rate. How much money are you going to lose
a month until you break even? Everybody thinks,
"Oh, we can break even in six months." That
means absolutely nothing to a VC or an angel
investor. They say, "Okay, great. What is your burn
rate?" If you don't know what they're talking
about, you will look like a knucklehead. The burn
rate might be $20k or $30k every month until you
get there and you show them how it will happen.

Don't be so sure they are going to freak out. Let's
say it is a $1-million deal and you are five months
away from being able to be profitable. It is going

to cost you $30,000 a month. If you are going to burn $150,000 before you are profitable, they will probably not freak out about that, if they feel like the upside is enough when you turn the corner and become profitable. They will freak out if you don't hit that profitability deadline. They may put a milestone right there that has a great, big brick on the string attached to it that whacks you right between the eyes if you don't make that one. This will be one of their first indicators

They are not going to just hand you a check for $1 million, usually. They will usually dole that money out in pieces as you need it. It is like a construction model. If you don't meet that first milestone on the first $150,000 they give you, they are liable to take control right there and install a new board. They may just shut the deal down completely and go, "Whew! Man, we got out of that and we only lost $150,000. We could have lost a million. This guy's is a knucklehead."

I mentioned earlier it is easy to get a deal again after you made one work. The inverse is also true. This is a relatively small industry. It is probably a lot smaller than you would think. Be sure when you quote that burn rate that it is accurate. It is probably one of the most important figures you can quote.

When Jeff Bezos did Amazon.com, they lost money for three years. They were burning millions a month for three years. On the very front end of his deal he said:

> "We're building the biggest store in the world. Eventually it is going to gross $2 or $3 million a year. It is a giant deal. We're going to burn up about $200 million, but we will end up making billions."

He convinced enough smart people and they said, "Okay, we're going to ride out the burn with you."

He communicated on the front end. If he hadn't, they would have crushed him. If he said, "We're going to be profitable in three months," he would have been out on his ear in the parking lot. There is no way they would have held onto him.

Don't tell them what you think they want to hear. Tell them what is going to happen. I would pad myself. If I think it's going to be four months, I'd give myself six. Go with the worst-case scenario. They will want to know about cost of insurance, if you have existing insurance policies and so forth. Really, they want to see here that you are smart enough to have thought about abating risk.

Disclose Everything

A lot of these deals fall apart not because of bad management or a bad product or a bad working business model. It is some liability that gets left over. The boss sexually harasses the secretary in the first year. She sues the company for $10 million and the company is only worth $1 million. You don't have any sexual harassment insurance. This is why they will look at your character so heavily. Maybe you have a wrongful discharge of an employee.

Maybe you have a technology that is not the same as Google but similar and Google decides that even though they might not win, they're going to sue you anyway and bury you in legal fees. This is the kind of stuff they will be looking for.

Are you kind of walking the line with what you are doing and how risky is that to blow up? Are you protecting yourself? Regulation compliance is huge. This is stuff like OSHA. If you are dealing with medical stuff it is FDA, EPA, and all the different, three-letter agencies. You need to absolutely disclose all your communications and correspondence with any regulatory agency. You need to bring licenses, regulatory certificates, and things like that. Give them all of that.

If you've been sued in the past or had criminal proceedings in the past, you or any of your key staff, you need to disclose that up front. It may blow your deal up. If you don't disclose it, it will definitely blow your deal up. They will find out. They are going to check you out thoroughly. Don't think, "Well, I'm going to hope to squeak by." It isn't going to happen, especially if this is about any real money. If you had a bankruptcy in the past, you definitely want to tell them about that. An in depth resume on the founder is really important. It should include past things you have done and accomplished, stuff you did in past businesses, if you tried other start-ups and failed. It is okay. If you tried other start-ups and failed with other people's money, that's a little less okay, but still not necessary going to knock you out. What will knock you out is not telling them.

Most entrepreneurs have fallen off the horse and gotten back on. That is a big benefit. Some entrepreneurs will fall off the horse and never get back on. At least you can prove you have resilience, as you said. You're not somebody who quits. You don't give up the first time you hit a dead end.

So you will know, here are some people they are going to talk to. They are probably going to talk to your employees. They are going to definitely going to talk to your employees. They may come in and talk to employees you were not planning on. This could be people that work in your warehouse or your phone center. "I'd like to talk to one of your phone center people privately. You don't mind, do you?" They are doing that to see how the leadership cascades down, but they are also looking for the truth from somebody who has not been prepped.

You and your key staff are going to all be singing from the same songbook. If they walk out in the warehouse and ask, "How's business?" they may hear, "We're not shipping much this week." "Really? How much did you ship this week?" "We shipped 50 cases." If you just told them that business was crazy and you are as busy as you can be, that is the guy they want to talk to. If you're not prepared, they will totally catch you off guard. They are going to talk to your board members. If you have an advisory board—something I really suggest you have—they will talk to your board members, the people who are advising you along the way. They will talk to your past investors, your small pool of investors. This will probably be okay. They are going to be cheerleaders for you.

They are going to talk to your competitors; there's a good chance they will. They might say, "Hey, I'm thinking of investing in some business. What do you think of this one?" They know the competitor is going to bash you out. They are looking for nuggets of truth in how the competitor is bashing you out.

They know the competitor is not going to say, "Oh, that guy is terrific. He has a wonderful product. We love him." They know better than that. They also know that this guy has a vested interested in tanking you, so they want to know his best piece of ammunition to tank you. Whatever he has is probably what all of your competitors have. It may show a vulnerability in your armor.

They will talk to the people you do business with. They will talk to former employees and former employers you have worked with in other businesses. They are definitely going to talk to your customers and your suppliers. You can bet on that.

They will talk to your references, but they don't put much weight on that, believe it or not. Nobody is going to put down a reference and say, "Talk to this guy. He hates me." Everybody puts down their pastor and their mom and their uncle in the insurance business. Those are no big deal, but they will probably talk to them. You might tell your references that what the VC is looking for is an enthusiastic response. If they call your references and they say nonchalantly, "Yeah, he's a pretty good guy," that will be quite a disappointment. They figure this guy is your cheerleader and he's the best you have. He needs to be telling them you're amazing. You shouldn't be anything less than miraculous to that person.

They will want to talk to your accountant, your attorney, and your other service providers. You will have to give permission to those professionals to talk to them. They are going to look at your team. What motivates them? What synergies do they have that work together? You can have individuals as a team and show the strength of the individuals, but it is a really great idea to have one sheet that shows why all these people can do miraculous things together that they can't do apart. How do they collaborate? What collective synergies do they have?

They will want to make sure that the backgrounds you give for all of your key employees are accurate. They will check them out. You need to let your key employees know that if they fluffed their resumes when they came to work for you, they need to defluff them before they are given to the VCs. They are going to run background checks. They will run pretty significant background checks on each of your key employees and a very extensive one on you.

They are going to look for your financial stability. They look at your credit rating not so much because they want to give you credit. They just want to see that you are a responsible person and that you are financially stable. If you are buried in credit card debt and buried in home debt, you can't pay your bills and all that, you are going to suck more money out of the business.

They are also interested in the quality of your personal life. They want you to have a stable personal life. They like married with family a lot. Even though single people will work crazy hours sometimes, married people are typically more committed, more stable, and more even keel. They are more motivated to get stuff done faster. Also, they tend to stick.

They want to know your commitment to the business. This is where all that work you are going to do ahead of time comes in. It is getting people together, scratching up all your money, and having your skin in the game. How committed are you to this thing? That is a really important factor. Another important factor is how committed your team is, too. "Jimmy, he's committed." Why? Usually the most committed people are there because they believe in what you are doing. It is not because of the money or the compensation. They believe in the mission of the company, whatever that is. Most smart people know that. People don't become committed to salaries. They get committed to a cause. Most of these guys are going to know that.

What Now? 16

The next thing is a big, old check. You're going to get your money, your funding, in whatever way they agreed to pay it out. It could be one chunk or in pieces over a period of time. That will happen pretty quickly. You will need a business bank account to put it in. You will need somebody that is a better bean counter than you are, unless you just happen to have an accounting background. Most entrepreneurs don't.

All you need to know is that after the deal they just want to know with transparency how you are managing the business day to day, how your progress is moving toward your goals and making sure you deliver all the reporting documents, the requirements they asked for on a very timely basis.

I love the idea of a blog, a private blog just between you and your investors. You can post every single day, "This is what happened today. We've moving toward the goal." If today was a setback, it was a setback. Maybe you have a smiley face and a frowning face. Tell them the good, the bad, and the ugly: tell them all of it. Especially tell them unexpected challenges. Here's big, gigantic, huge mistake #47. Something catastrophic comes up; in your mind something comes up that just wrecks your business plan. You don't tell your investor and you bury your head in the sand hoping it fixes itself somehow before it is time for the next report. The very best thing you can do is pick up the phone right then, call your angel investor or your VC investor and say, "We just hit a brick wall." They may very well know a way through or around that wall that you won't think of.

Use your resources. In most cases your heart is going to ache and you're going to feel like a failure, but they are going to lose a lot of money. That's important. A lot of times, they have more to lose than you do, so they have a definite vested interest in trying to help you overcome that obstacle as quickly as they possibly can.

The only other thing I can tell you is to start working toward your exit strategy. Start working with them. Things are going well and you would like to meet once a month or once a quarter and starting talking about exit strategies and what the best one might be. This means you can either go public, which is a biggy; you could get acquired which means you merge with another company with cash and stock or whatever. You could just sell outright. Somebody might come and say, "I'll give you $10 million cash," and you sell. You could have some sort of a buyout like where you buy out your investors or your investors buy out you.

One thing people overlook a lot of franchising. Franchising is a form of exit strategy. You decide you are going to build a franchise company out of this proven model you have and let all kinds of other business owners fund your national growth for a share. You never think of franchising as a form of funding, you never think of it as an exit strategy, but it really is. You are basically selling your company to a series of dealers. That is pretty much what you can expect after the sale.

Troubleshooting 17

When things are not going right, when you're not getting appointments, when you're not getting interest when you pitch.

Bad Ideas

I have a friend by the name of Marlon Sanders. He is one of the coolest guys I've ever known and he is a marketing genius. He has a saying. He says, "Dead ducks don't quack."

Sometimes, the greatest idea in the world to you is just a bad idea. The market is not right for it, the timing is not right for it, there is already too much competition. There is some reason. Basically, your business concept may just be flawed.

I hate to see people argue with experts and that's what people tend to do. They say, "You don't understand this and this. Mine is different." If you're talking to pretty wise people, yours isn't different. They've seen hundreds of them. You may need to listen to that counsel. You might go back and tuck your tail between your legs.

Remember what I said? If you win, you win big. If you fail, you fail big once you're funded. One of the worst things that can happen to you is to get funded with a flawed model. It is one of the worst things that can happen to you because it can totally ruin your track record. You're a sunken ship that never gets off of the ocean floor.

Bad Pitch Men

One thing is that not everybody is a great presenter; everybody is not a great pitch man. Do you know the story of the Woz? Steve Wozniak was the guy who invented the Apple computer. He was the brains behind Apple and the brains behind everything that had to do with Apple Computer for many years. He was an extremely shy introvert. He got some funding from Hewlett Packard, I think. He got $10,000 or $50,000 and one of the coolest things he did with his first paycheck was to go buy a gold chain. A technology grant is all he got; it wasn't really funding. He went to the mall in California and there was a guy at a kiosk selling jewelry in this mall. The guy did a terrific job at selling him this gold chain and he remembered it.

Somewhere along the line a little while later, he was trying to present his ideas to some people and they just didn't understand. They said, "Son, you need to get somebody in here who knows how to sell and to explain what you have." He went back to the mall and he asked the guy behind the counter selling gold chains if he wanted to be his partner. That guy was Steve Jobs. That's how Apple Computer started. Steve Jobs was the ultimate pitch man.

You may need to get somebody else to do the presentation for you. That might not be your cup of tea and that's okay. A lot of times people's egos get in the way. "This is my company! I built this thing from nothing!" and on and on and on. You can either have 100% of a tiny, little pond or you can have a great big spot in a giant ocean. It is kind of up to you. An ego will limit you greatly, always, in everything you do, particularly in funding and the growth of a start-up business.

Broke Investors

This is one that is pretty common: you find yourself talking to broke people. You're either talking to people that don't have the money to fund you if they wanted to or people who are really not even in your genre of funding. Most companies don't do their due diligence, their homework. They get the phone book out and look up a list of all the venture capital companies and start calling them. "I'm going to set up appointments and pitch them." You have a Web 2.0 application for the Internet and these guys fund medical projects. Maybe you have a great medical project and they fund real estate projects.

Almost all of these companies specialize because they usually have industry experts on staff. That is what makes a good VC. If you are in the medical instruments business and you find a VC company with a couple of guys on the board that are retired from Metronics or Schering-Plough Corporation or Pfizer. They probably know a little about the business. They probably know a lot of people in the business. They can open great, big doors. One of my favorite sayings in the world: Little, bitty hinges swing great, big doors. You never know who can open that door for you.

Make sure you are talking to the right people. Don't waste a lot of your time. If you are just practicing, that's fine. However, sometimes it can be discouraging. If a person can't fund your deal, they're not going to say, "Hey, I'd love to fund your deal, but I'm broke." They will probably pick your deal apart just to have an excuse not to fund it. It makes you feel bad; it makes you worry. You go back and change a bunch of stuff that maybe didn't need to be changed. That's one thing.

Unfundable Deals

Sometimes you don't have a fundable deal. You don't have a deal that has a big enough market, that has enough penetration that a VC company can reach into their pocket, pull out their money, and expect a reasonable return of investment. It is not that you don't have a great idea. Maybe it is just a great idea for a small business and maybe you need to run it as a small business. Spend your own money; raise some money from family and friends. Run it as a small business and that's cool.

We live in Austin, Texas. There is some wicked, cool stuff in Austin, Texas, because there are some wicked, cool people in Austin, Texas. Go, Austin, Texas! However, there is some stuff in Austin, Texas, that wouldn't work in Salina, Kansas. There is some kind of super hipster stuff that just wouldn't fly in the Midwest; it wouldn't fly in Ohio and Pennsylvania. Okay, now I'm going to get hate mail. "Are you saying Pennsylvania is not cool?" I'm not saying that. I'm just saying that this is a college-type of environment and certain things that work here may not work somewhere else. There is a lot of stuff in Pennsylvania that is really nice and works there that would totally probably flop in Austin for whatever reason. I might be that you take a deal in and say, "I have my super trendy Eel Cooked 17 Ways Restaurant." It's killing them in Austin because people want to try anything new and different. That's great, but they are probably not going to be downing that eel too heavily in Owasso, Oklahoma. You may be able to go to New York, L.A., Chicago, or San Francisco, but you will have a capped market audience. There might not be a big enough market for whatever you are doing.

The Wrong Team

One of the things might be that your team is incomplete. You just don't have the right people on the team. I've repeated this a couple of times, but it's worth repeating. You just need to have a good financial person; that is really super-important.

The Bad Pitch

Something may have gone wrong with your presentation. Perhaps your slides were out of order, you showed the wrong things, you didn't give the information they really needed. You wouldn't believe how many pitches never really clarify. I've seen tons of VC pitches: after thirty minutes of talking and fifteen minutes of slides, the investor is just going, "I don't get it." You just failed to make your point. What do you do? What is your competitive edge?

Here's the thing: you need to be able to say in one or two sentences clearly what you do.

Other Problems

Watch your milestones. I've really dumped it out there. They fail because they don't have good business plans. They focus on the product rather than the business model or the market. They underestimate investors. They won't ask for stuff and they try to hide things from them. They don't prepare at all for due diligence and when they get into due diligence they find out what they were told was total guesswork. They don't have the right investors.

These are things that go wrong with deals. Just know this going in.

That is pretty much it.

I really wish you a lot of luck. Just be honest and make sure you have something really good and unique before you go. Go out online and search sample business plans and sample funding deals.

There are a lot of websites. You can register on some of the angel investor sites as an investor.

Sometimes they ask you qualifying questions and sometimes they don't. If you can register on a site as an investor, a lot of times they will show you the deals that have been read the most. Those are the ones that are most appealing to the investors. Find out what the common denominators are there. Pick out the pieces of each one that are consistent. Pick out the ones that have been read the least and do the same. Get an idea of a complete package and what seems to be working and what is not working.

With what you've learned so far, go back and read this again. Start small: start with your own money, start with your investor club. Keep in constant communication all the way through the process. A blog is really an awesome way to keep up with your little investors, big investors, and your medium-sized investors. Communication is the key. It is absolutely the key to making the process flow. With this information, you should be able to go out within thirty days or so and probably raise all the money you need to fund any really viable business.

Good luck to you. Please contact us through the website listed at the front of this book. Send us your success stories, your questions, your failures, and all the above. Please keep in contact with us. We would love to hear your stories of how you're doing. Thank you, again, for investing in this course.

Index

437

www.ingramcontent.com/pod-product-compliance
Lightning Source LLC
Chambersburg PA
CBHW022049210326
41519CB00054B/287

* 9 7 8 1 9 3 7 1 2 6 9 9 5 *